ON THE BOARD

Geoffrey Mills MBE

Gower
in association with
the Institute of Directors

Published by
Gower Publishing Company Limited,
Gower House, Croft Road, Aldershot,
Hampshire GU11 3HR, England.

British Library Cataloguing in Publication Data

Mills, Geoffrey
  On the board.
  1. Directors of corporations
  I. Title
  658.4'2   HD2745

  ISBN 0-566-02260-5

Typeset by Pintail Studios Ltd, Ringwood, Hants
Printed and bound in Great Britain by
Billing and Sons, Guildford

ON THE BOARD

Contents

Preface

My interest in the realities of Boardroom performance was first aroused when sitting on a bad Board composed of good men. Its features are reflected, in differing patterns, in many other Boardrooms. The performance of groupings of men will always depend on their mix, the depth of their commitment, and how they are led.

The ideal requirements of all Boards are fundamentally similar. This book can thus seek to be helpful to managers and directors in companies of all shapes and sizes.

It writes about 'men' for ease of reading. Women, who are often as sharp and more true, could make good directors if they first had the chance to develop some management experience.

My own experience, and my justification for writing at all, is varied. As an executive and non-executive director on public, private, holding, divisional and subsidiary Boards, and today as a management consultant, I have had close involvement with a variety of companies. Before moving into business management I was educated or experienced as a scientist, colonial administrator, diplomat, trade commissioner and magistrate, working in most corners of the world.

Thus if some of the suggestions on the following pages seem unconventional, it could be because I perceive this most critically important question of Boardroom performance from a number of unconventional viewpoints.

Or because, on the evidence of the record, the conventional viewpoint has not always been the most effective.

Geoffrey Mills
Claygate, Esher

1 The Board is . . .

The Board is . . .
responsible.
Those who appoint it enjoy the protection of a most lenient
limited liability.
The Board itself has no similar legal lifebelt.

It is . . .
an anomaly in law.
Its directors are agents of the company, but are neither agents
nor servants of the shareholders who appoint them.
They are bound by the company's own Memorandum and
Articles, and by a widening shelf-ful of national legislation,
which describe the extent to which the Board is responsible.

It is . . .
an entity separate from the sum of its individual directors,
which makes single collective decisions.
It can evolve and change as an entity in step with the changing
demands of its company's growth stages and business
environment.
It can remain wiser than its wisest director, or fail more
foolishly than its weakest, in accordance with how well it
does evolve and change to meet those demands.

It is . . .
infinitely variable.
There are few constraints on its composition, and none on its
style.

It is . . .
the company's final arbiter.
It makes the first and the last decisions, and unmakes any

earlier or down-line decisions which it later judges differently.

The lifespan and vigour of its company become good, or bad, or depressingly mediocre, in accordance with the wisdom and intent with which the Board makes and monitors its decisions.

The Board alone has ultimate responsibility for corporate standards of performance.

It is . . .
the company's top manager.

It is appointed to control the company, which means to direct and manage the management, who in turn control the sum of its business operations.

Its prime responsibilities are therefore:

- to evaluate, define, and when necessary re-define, the businesses in which the company will operate, the resources which will be allocated to each, and the timing and rates of return which are required from each;
- to select, monitor, and hold responsible the managers to whom the daily control of these operations is entrusted. Particularly, but not exclusively, the Chief Executive.

Companies fail when their Boards do not discharge effectively either one, or both, of these overriding responsibilities. Which occurs when:

- the Board itself is poorly led or uniformly composed, seeks rest rather than a continuing restlessness, looks comfortably inward rather than critically outward and forward; or when
- the selection of, or subsequent failure to remove, inadequate managers is based on dominant individual objectives, not corporate objectives; or is based on blinkering, or blindness, or both.

The Board is . . .
a counsellor.

It does not wait passively to evaluate the operational or planning proposals which come up to it in neat packages, but actively advises and assists where possible in their compilation.

There is no law nor Article which states that it must do this.

There are no regulations nor precedents which prescribe limits on how much or how little the directors can be charged by the Board to undertake, nor how deep or shallow these undertakings can be.

As the entity responsible for controlling the company, it should not need legislation to explain to it that it must be active rather than acquiescent.

It is . . .

the keeper of the company's conscience and the measure of corporate morality.

It sets the standards of corporate courage, and thereby delimits the management's morale.

From the Boardroom to the shopfloor, both productivity and performance are most closely affected by morale, which is itself most closely affected by visible morality.

The effective company meets its creditors on time, especially the small ones; does not abuse its suppliers nor maltreat its physical environment; is clinically correct with its customers, employees, auditors, analysts, shareholders, lenders and taxmen.

While there is little room or requirement for altruism within the competitive corporation, there are very few corporate employees who find it satisfying to break any of the rules.

It is . . .

a group, programmed with the psychology and dynamics which govern the behaviour of all human groupings, from humble to great.

In this it is as far removed from the psychology and dynamics of its individual directors as an ant-hill is from its ants, or a coral reef from one of its polyps.

Boards can fail, and so companies can fail, when these characteristics are ignored, not known, or denied.

And it is . . .

performing poorly.

It is today acknowledged in the UK and USA, by those who study Boards from within and without, that companies:

are failing to keep pace with their changing environments;

are producing declining real returns on resources
deployed;

are contributing at a declining rate to the net creation of
wealth.

Within Continental Europe performance has maintained a
brisker momentum. The European has better marshalled and
managed his resources to meet business conflict openly –
whether it be external conflict in the market-place, or internal
conflict in the relationships between managers and managed.

In the UK, the two major miracles of gas and oil have not
altered this trend. In the USA, the dynamism which had long
been powered by its own much more varied natural resources
begins to dissipate.

A national performance is essentially the sum of corporate
performance, which is itself a summing of individual Board
performances. The performance of a Board can be very
different from the intrinsic quality of its company's businesses,
or from the professional quality of its individual directors.
Witness the major corporate disasters of recent decades,
where Boards magnificent with men of undeniable quality
have dropped into the rubble of their companies, almost
before they detected that something was wrong with the
edifices they so splendidly straddled. Germany in the 1930s,
the USA in the 1950s and 1960s, Italy and the UK, even
Japan, in the 1960s and 1970s – there is no lack of well-
publicised examples, as well as a whole host of smaller
dissolutions which never triggered public comment. The
directors were splendid, but their companies crumbled with as
much dignity as the walls of Jericho, not because the directors
suddenly all went crazy, but because their Boards had
collectively failed. The directors had proved no more effective
as a Board than any dozen of their least experienced shareholders or junior managers could have been, given the chance.

More important than the major corporate disasters of the
past is the progressive decline in total real performance of the
thousands of companies which continue to survive, their

declining progress disguised by a long period of inflation, which buoys up their apparent results. Many subsidiaries, for example, are already technically insolvent, but are carried along by their parent companies with guarantees or loans which no external lender would ever countenance.

The Board is an entity with many powers, but with demonstrably declining power. Not declining because the quality of directors or managers decreases – though it has been argued that most of the business schools in the world are not producing better businessmen. Not declining because directors and managers work less hard – though it is quite evident that many lose heart, sit tight, keep mum, and develop such a low profile that it is not just their heads which go under the sand. Others indeed work harder than they need, travel a very great deal more than they should, and burn more midnight oil than is good for them. But declining because the manner in which most Boards define what needs deciding and doing, the manner in which they monitor the achievement of what they have decided, and, most critically, the manner in which Boards compose themselves in the first place, is a hundred years behind the demands of the present increasingly competitive business environment.

The decline of the board is a universal phenomenon of this century.
PETER F. DRUCKER

Decision making by the Board is one of the few aspects of present-day management which cannot be computerised. The Board's collective work is all done in the minds of individual people. The quality and suitability of its work depends not only on the quality of the directors, but on how that group of people reacts with, stimulates, holds back, adds to or subtracts from each other. The Board is a group.

Psychology of groups

Current knowledge of the psychology and dynamics of groups, in which the individual subdues a part of his individuality in order to contribute to the collective activities of the group, is still limited.

Management aspects of group processes, even the hum-drum question of how to make committees more generally productive, have been little researched in comparison with all other aspects of management.

But a number of consistent conclusions about group effectiveness have been reached in studies conducted in several countries, and they do provide strong guidelines for compos-ing and controlling Boardroom groupings which can best meet the variety of responsibilities which are placed on the Board. If the reader who is also a Director compares these rather dry experimental conclusions with the details of his own Boardroom's behaviour, he will find all manner of parallels with features which disturb him about that behaviour.

Broadly:

- Groups produce better solutions to problems or tasks than individuals.
- Heterogeneous groups produce better solutions than homogeneous groups, than groups composed of people of similar styles and backgrounds. They are measurably more creative when the tasks to be achieved are complex.
- But for maximum effectiveness, the size of groups must be as small as can cover the variety of contributions required.
- The members who arrive at the best solutions to problems or tasks are most often in an initial minority. The success of a Board, as a group, must therefore lie in the facility and freedom with which members can influence each other, and with which the initial distinc-tions between majorities and minorities can be made to disappear, or become unimportant.
- The effectiveness of the group increases if it contains a clear leader, by character a self-confident decision maker. His natural role within the group is to ensure that individual members contribute what they can to the for-mation of a common decision. This requires him to trim back those who seek to domineer, including himself. Many a Chairman in a Board, and many a Chief Execu-tive in a management committee, finds difficulty in

differentiating between domineering and leading. Many an executive Director can recall with discomfort those management meetings which always proceeded as a monologue.

- The leader's ability to influence is closely correlated with his ability to be influenced. The leader who seeks to make all the decisions himself, rather than to maximise performance of the group, will produce progressively worse decisions as the potential contribution of his colleagues is withheld in frustration.

- There is a marked difference in the effectiveness of different styles of leadership. The 'domineering' leader produces a temporarily firmer behaviour within the group, but individual contribution declines. The group becomes less able to make collective decisions, works poorly together, loses morale. These may indeed be the very characteristics which satisfy the personal pre-ferences of the natural autocrat, but they do not meet the requirements and responsibilities of the group as a whole. The 'retiring' leader, who only offers his own opinions when asked for them, induces other members to show more initiative, but the group slowly loses both morale and its feeling of common responsibility. The 'democratic' leader actively helps individual members to focus on group objectives. Collective involvement develops, and the group becomes an effective separate entity.

- In groups where cohesion between the members is based on personal 'attraction' or similarity, discussion turns to gentle pleasantry. Where cohesion is based on the maintenance of the group's 'prestige' or 'standing', then the group strains to avoid any damage to its 'status' or 'acceptability'. Other objectives become subordinated to the pursuit of this non-productive aim. One member comes to dominate, and the others become submissive.

- On the other hand, where cohesion is based on the primary objective of task-achievement, then the conduct of affairs becomes more goal-oriented and businesslike. Thus the cohesiveness best suited to the enjoyment of, say, club membership, is quite different from the type best suited to the productive direction of a competitive enterprise. In the former (and many Boards are run on the principles of the nicest clubs) a drive to maintain cohesiveness will soon enough cross purposes with a drive to improve performance, and the objective of apparent cohesion will be sustained at the expense of effectiveness.

- Pressure for conformity (which most directors will immediately recognise as being a characteristic of their own Boardroom) can rob the group of original contribution. Where the issue on which there is strong disagreement is subjective, for example when it concerns individual people and their positions, the pressure exerted on the minority, or on the individual, becomes very great. Every executive Director with any length of experience will remember, with embarrassment or pain, a number of occasions in his career when he felt forced to acquiesce in a decision which he knew in his mind and in his bones to be 'wrong' – and which the passage of time has certainly demonstrated to have been wrong.

- In the homogeneous group of similar members with similar backgrounds, such pressure will normally whittle down the minority to one, and he will then have to choose whether to row in or to ride out. Prolonged non-conformity, particularly if seen normally in one member, is viewed by that kind of group as a threat. The greater the extent or the length of the non-conformity, the progressively less tolerant the other members become. Pressure grows from patient discussion, through terse comment, to impatience, to gentle ridicule, and then to abuse. (It happens like this in all groups, not just in the Boardroom.) Non-conformity creates anxiety, and the uniform group does not like the boat to be rocked. Even though the boat be becalmed, or sinking.

- The uniform or homogeneous group can produce effective decisions both rapidly and smoothly when the problems concerned are not particularly complex – in a business sense, when the trading environment is relatively stable. Thus the uniform Board was able to play its role with broadly adequate success in past decades. But the competitive environment is no longer stable, and never will be again. It will continue to exhibit increasingly rapid change. The tasks which face the Boardroom will continue to be complex and conflict-ridden.

Compatibility is not always a boon. In competitive situations it is measurably a disadvantage.

The Board as an effective group

In the knowledge that most, or all, of these characteristics apply as much to the Board as to any other human group, we can sketch the outline of a Board which has the best chance of remaining effective in a changeful competitive environment.

The effective Board is ...

1 heterogeneous; composed of people of markedly different styles and backgrounds.
2 flexible; composed primarily of people who are independent within the Board, and who are not bound by any firm allegiances inside it – neither to chum, nor to boss, nor to loyal subordinate. There will thus be no permanent majority or minority, and discussion will be characterised by the ad hoc grouping and regrouping of Directors to argue whichever case happens to make best sense. In practical terms, this means having a sufficient number of 'active' non-executive or outside Directors, who can detect when minority proposals are being suppressed, and who can 'side' with the non-conformists at least long enough for the Board to determine whether the minority proposal is 'better' or not. This is one of the most important Boardroom roles of the non-executive, and one which few of the current style of one-day-per-month men can even begin to play.
3 task-oriented; discussion being centred on achieving specific and common objectives, not simply on reaching broad-brush political or policy conclusions. Such conclusions will always prove sterile

unless followed by the definition of related action and performance goals. These enable the Directors to identify with the Board's measured objectives, to become committed to its measurable success, and eventually to feel that success or failure is their own success or failure. It is not enough that Directors are legally responsible. They must both feel, and want to be, responsible.

4   performance-oriented; achievement must be regularly analysed, explained, redirected. The knowledge of real success improves morale, which in turn improves productivity.

5   free of all non-combatants. It has been experimentally determined (though every Director already knows this in his toes) that the regular non-contributor has a distinctly unsettling effect within small groups.

6   small. A Board of more than about ten Directors will become stiff with non-combatants.

7   led democratically – so that each Director's opinion may be freely presented and impartially judged.

8   a clique, not a claque.

2 The Board is not . . .

The Board is not . . .
a Club.
Companionship and convenience do not feature in its
  objectives.

A study published in 1974 ('Commonalities and Connections among Directors of Large Financial Institutions',
Richard Whitley, Manchester Business School) recorded
some striking data regarding the composition of the Boards of
27 of the largest City companies. While the high correlation
discovered between actual club membership and Oxbridge
College background might well have been expected, the high
level of interwoven directorships between the 27 companies, of
interwoven blood relationships between the 27 Boards, and of
common schooling among the Directors must cause considerable surprise.

Not less than 46 of the Directors of the Boards of the 8
leading insurance companies in the sample had been schooled
at Eton, an average of almost 6 Eton Directors apiece. And 34
per cent of the whole sample of 341 Directors on whom data
were available had been educated at that same school.
However undoubtedly excellent one school and its products
may be, the statistical odds against such percentage composition resulting from any criterion other than clubbability are
remote.

The Board is empowered and entitled to compose itself in
any way which it judges fit, and which the shareholders in
General Meeting will endorse. And the Boards covered in the
Whitley study, which included the largest clearing banks,
merchant banks, discount houses and insurance companies,

11

have succeeded through recent years in preserving the inter-national pre-eminence of the City in their particular fields of activity (with notable hiccups in the mid-1970s). Looking forward however through changing years, it will be interesting to observe whether the composition of the Boards of these large financial institutions will shift significantly, and whether British market share in these fields will continue to be pre-served. Given the technical expertise of these institutions, there is no current reason why it should not be preservable.

But clubbability can also have its ridiculous aspects. Con-sider a case described to the writer concerning a publicly-quoted Group which was expanding in good markets. A succession of head-hunting organisations had strained unsuccessfully to search out an acceptable new Chief Execu-tive designate to take over, in a short period, from the ageing incumbent. Eventually, through the expedient of once traditional recruitment advertising, an appropriate man was located and selected. But before the die was cast by the desig-nated himself, the Chairman took the man aside and advised bluntly that the soon-to-retire incumbent would never let the designated succeed him because the new man was not a Freemason. So several more head-hunters and advertisers had to be brought in before another year's passage located the right sort of chap who gave the right sort of handshake.

In a small private organisation one might almost understand, though not freely accept, this level of required clubbability. In a significant publicly-quoted corporation it smacks of the very grossest irresponsibility. And yet, dig a little and you will find many similarities. There are many kinds of clan and club and coterie among men.

The Board is not . . .
a committee.
Committees are set up by other bodies, which give them terms
    of reference. The Board continuously defines and redefines
    its own terms of reference. It should not, therefore, accept
    and trot through the agenda presented to it on the sole
    initiative of the Chairman, or of the Chief Executive, or of
    the two in tandem. It should, on the initiative of the
    Directors as a whole, combine in compiling its own agenda.

This is the least awkward way of defining detailed terms of reference, without having to repeat to the Chairman, or Chief Executive, or both, that they must not seek to cover only those questions which they are personally prepared to cover.

The Board may not acquiesce on the nod. It may not, committee-wise, conceive camels of compromise through comfortable consensus.

The Board is not . . .
a formality.
It is not a programme of ten or twelve meetings per annum (worse, three or four) at which a series of tidy agenda are tidily despatched.
It is not a rubber-stamp for decisions in practice already made, nor, worse, for actions already taken, though it is often treated as such – particularly in those countries which apply a two-tier system of Board in which the 'upper' tier cannot in reality have any other purpose. This is also true in the UK, where many a chairman will take it as a personal affront when Directors express disagreement with a pre-digested decision which is dropped onto the Board table for rapid ratification. Among the many detailed characteristics of Boardroom behaviour in less than successful companies, this is perhaps the most prevalent. At least it is the most visible.

This is surprising if we pause to consider that even Karl Marx was able to determine that life is all about 'conflict'. The very essence of business life, in particular, is complexity, competition, and conflict. If it was not absolutely inevitable that there could be significant disagreement in the Boardroom on one item or another on the agenda about every second or third meeting, then one would not need the Board at all. If there is no air of tension as one enters the Boardroom about every second or third meeting, then one can safely conclude that the Board is becoming too remote from the conflict of the arenas in which its corporate performance is being determined. Certainly the Boardroom should not become a battlefield where the factions sally out from under their respective banners, fighting for what each banner represents and then rallying back to it after every skirmish. But if it does not experience a painful skirmish every now and again, it is probably already dead.

The Board is not . . .
an ivory tower, remote from or largely uninterested in its managers and their managing.
The success of the Board's decision in the field depends as much on the managers' ability or opportunity to implement as on the wisdom of the original decision. The field failure of a Board policy, whether because it is badly implemented or because it was a bad decision to begin with, can seldom be exposed to the Board in sufficient time to make suitable adjustments if the Board works to a watertight separation from management. It has been demonstrated that in many of the major corporate collapses of recent years, the problems of the companies concerned were not clearly known to their Boards until very shortly before, or sometimes after, they sank. A few months before Rolls-Royce collapsed its Board stated publicly that 'The company is in good shape'.

The smaller the company, the less distinct the borderline between policy and management, and there is precious little difference at all when the unit contains less than 300–400 employees.

Remoteness from management at any size will mean that the practicality of Board decisions will be about as dependable as doing the football pools blindfold.

3   *Pressures on the Board*

Boards have come into the spotlight in the USA and the UK. They will remain there, and the light will intensify, until such time as they have evolved, or had imposed on them, a style and a structure which satisfies a motley of special interests: governments, trade unions, employees, consumers – and maybe even shareholders and lenders, should these also evince a similar level of interest.

The pressures on Boards are part natural and external. They are also in part the result of an increasing exposure by these special interest groupings of features in current Board performance, or behaviour, which each respective grouping considers unacceptable.

In the first case:

- developing competition from developing and developed countries, both Eastern and Western;
- developing international technology;
- the evolution of individual markets;
- the cost, or availability, or sourcing of funding and capital, and
- the political and material demands of populations.

In the second case:

- a series of UK Department of Trade reports which have indicated that all is not sweet and true in all Boardrooms, paralleled by a series of similar reported findings in the USA;
- a combination of inflation, recession and new thinking on accounting techniques, which has led the analysts to do their sums differently, and to conclude that, in real terms, the net performance of most companies has been

declining for years, irrespective of what their press handouts have stated. Professor Gerald Lawson of the Manchester Business School has calculated that in 16 of the years from 1954–76 the distribution to shareholders by companies using historic cost accounting had exceeded equity earnings, and had to be financed by borrowings (see Appendix III);

— a flailing-about by the power groups of government and trade unions to find means of ensuring that the employees' growing anxieties can be solved. Their arguments for corporate change are weak, but the UK's comparative performance has been so poor that corporate counter-arguments can sound even weaker.

In this chapter we review briefly the pressures which are forcing the demand for corporate change. Some of these pressures lie equally heavily on governments; some are created by them.

The increasing danger is that if Boards do not restyle and revitalise at their own initiative then governments will stumble in to try to do it for them.

Markets and competition

UK Boards have been stating publicly since 1978 that the strength of the £ is adversely affecting their international performance. The £ has in fact fallen for many years in comparison with the currencies of competitor countries (see Figure 3.1). Against a time-scale which is short in terms of the life-spans of companies, it remains low in comparison with all except the currency of the USA, where Boards and corporate performance are also in the spotlight.

In the mid-1950s UK share of world trade in manufactured products was about 25 per cent, with Germany holding well under 20 per cent and Japan under 5 per cent. Today the UK share is under 10 per cent, with Germany holding over 20 per cent and Japan over 15 per cent. In this period the deutsche mark and the yen have risen, but the £ has dropped. *Der*

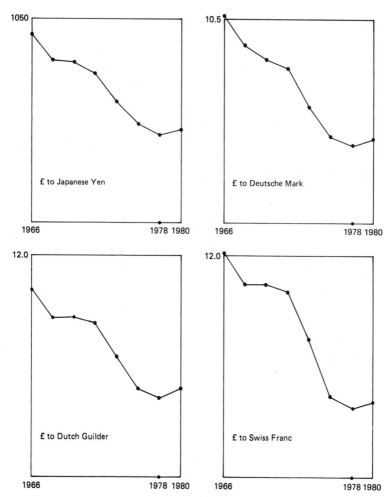

Figure 3.1 Strength of the £ against selected foreign currencies, 1966–80

Spiegel recorded in 1977, when the £ was nearing its lowest ebb, that:

In 1976 France's gross national product was one and a half times that of Great Britain and the Federal Republic's was twice as large. The country which for centuries was dependent on trade, last year exported goods to the value of just $46,000 million, hardly more than the Netherlands with only a quarter of the British population. In the same year the Federal Republic exported goods to the value of $102,000 million.

At the time of that article most British Boards (plus the media, banks, government, and everyone else) were saying that the £ was too low. It took only one year for the arguments to reverse. It is today a tenet of faith in most Boardrooms that if the government would only let the value of the £ drop a bit more, then the UK could do better in overseas markets. Their attention focuses on the £'s rise against the US dollar. But it cannot make economic or business sense to downgrade the £ more, just because another currency is weakening.

The arguments against devaluation are always relevant:

- A 10 per cent devaluation coupled with price reductions overseas requires an 11 per cent increase in volume to regain the same intake of foreign currency. Such overall volume increase seldom results quickly enough to have any net positive effect.
- Devaluation increases the import bill overnight, and the anticipated benefits of import substitution do not reach the desired volume. Witness the rate of increase of imports into the UK since the years of the £'s steepest decline.
- Devaluation thus feeds inflation. Witness the countless UK companies reporting losses in the late-1970s on large overseas contracts which were obtained with the artificial aid of a depressed £ in the mid-1970s.
- The lead-time for increases in sales of industrial products and major plant projects, on which the UK trade balance so greatly depends, is measured in years.
- The levelling-up of costs in this period eliminates the anticipated pricing flexibility.
- The UK employee can still claim to be worse paid than his European counterpart, even though wage and salary increases in the UK have been very much greater, in each of several successive years, than in Europe. The rate of increase is disguised by the relative fall in the UK currency.

Devaluation has one far more insidious effect. It 'allows for' a decline in competitiveness when Boards should, instead, be concentrating on how to overcome that decline.

Compare Germany. As the deutsche mark rose steadily, increasing pressure on their overseas pricing, German Boards focused on those other factors in the competitive equation which induce customers to buy: reliability, design, service, delivery, distribution. By remorselessly improving productivity they steadily forced down unit costs so that, irrespective of the continuing rise of their currency, they could maintain price competitiveness as well. At unemployment levels and inflation rates both strikingly less than those of the UK.

Devaluation enables Boards to take their eye, momentarily, off the ball with which their games are being played. Those games are contested in worldwide markets. Yet a study in 1975 ('Concentration on Key Markets: A Development Plan for Exports', ITI Research) demonstrated that small UK companies had twice as many salesmen covering the UK as they had covering the rest of the world. And large UK companies had eight times as many home salesmen as they had covering the rest of the world. True, the picture is a little complicated by the use of overseas agents, subsidiaries and licensing, but it remains fact that companies in Japan and Germany employ several times as many export salesmen as British companies of equivalent size. Further, they concentrate their attack on a smaller number of specified markets, deploying comprehensive sales teams in those markets until they have achieved a dominant market share. If UK Boards planned to win overseas markets with similar intensity, we would not need to worry about the currency.

As the French Prime Minister stated in 1980: 'It is not a question of adapting the franc to the needs of business, but one of business adapting its requirements to the needs of the franc'.

Technology and population

Pressure to apply new technology, in order to remain competitive and thereby continue in business, coincides, worldwide, with a pressure to maintain employment for populations which do not decrease in step with the decreasing requirement for employees (see Figure 3.2).

There are three mutually conflicting factors:

- populations do not decrease;
- populations will not accept a standstill in living standards;
- increasing worldwide technology enables all countries to produce more with fewer people.

This technology is being applied more slowly in the UK than in competitor countries. The competitors' costs go down; their market share therefore goes up; which means that their unit costs can come down again; which means that their market share goes up again. And so on. Meanwhile the UK continues to produce less efficiently; competes less effectively; sells less; produces less; maintains employment through over-manning.

Japan has come closest to maintaining a balance between the three mutually conflicting factors. Its share of world trade has risen from 30 per cent of the UK's share in the late 1950s to 150 per cent of the UK's current share. Its population has increased at the same time from 93 to 115 million, yet its unemployment has only risen from 0.9 per cent to 1.8 per cent in the period. It has steadily improved local living standards. While it is now widely known that Japan is no longer a country of cheap labour – its average income exceeding that of the UK – it is still widely believed that Japan produces little of the technology which it so avidly applies.

Not so. The number of scientists and engineers employed on research and development in Japan rose from 1969–77 by 48 per cent. In Germany the rise was 39 per cent, in the UK it was scarcely noticeable, and in the USA it was zero (*UNESCO Yearbook*, 1980). In the first half of the 1970s Japanese patent applications rose by 40 per cent, while the UK registered a decrease of 12 per cent. In 1977, the latest year for which data are available from the World Intellectual Property Organisation, Japanese patent applications within Japan exceeded the total of resident patent applications in the US plus Germany plus the UK by 19 per cent.

Another Far Eastern dynamo, Singapore, is methodically

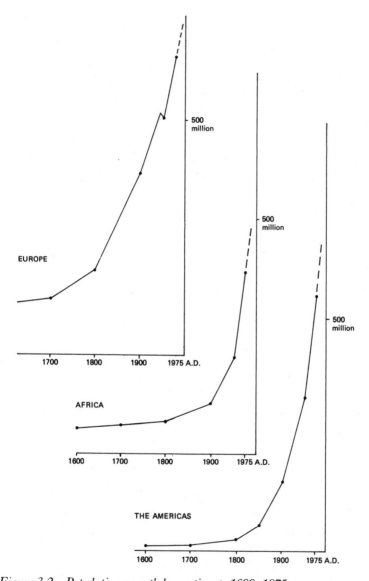

Figure 3.2   Population growth by continent, 1600–1975

Source: Reprinted and adapted by permission of Penguin Books Ltd., Colin McEvedy and Richard Jones, *Atlas of World Population History*, Penguin Reference Books, 1978, pp. 18, 206, 270. Copyright © Colin McEvedy and Richard Jones, 1978.

moving up market in the application of technology. It is also tackling its population problem, with fiscal and other disincentives to achieve a nil growth rate by AD 2030. Only the Chinese could seriously plan 50 years ahead. The plan already works. Truly resolute planning usually does.

Attila the Hun and the Vikings demonstrated what humans do when the pressure of bodies becomes greater than the home economy can handle. And lemmings demonstrate what some animals do in similar circumstances. Boards cannot do anything about the circumstances. But they will only worsen them if they continue to lose market share. The pressure to apply technology as it becomes available, or to create it, cannot be responsibly resisted. Corporate survival, for which the Board is responsible, depends on doing this against all contrary pressures.

Productivity and power groups

GEC is one of the most successful manufacturing groups in the UK. Its turnover doubled in the last 5 years as it reduced its employees by 10,000. Yet Siemens of Germany, a major competitor, achieves three times the turnover of GEC with only 75 per cent more employees. And General Electric of the USA, another major competitor, generates twice GEC's turnover per employee. Comparisons worsen when made against less competent UK companies.

To explain such wide discrepancies by concluding that UK companies have invested less per employee in modern production plant gives only part of an answer, and one which is not always relevant, even in part. In the last 5 years ICI has spent more on plant modernisation than any other international chemicals company, and has reduced its employees by almost 50,000. Yet value added per employee in the UK chemicals industry, which is dominated by ICI, remains less than half that achieved in Germany, and a quarter that achieved in the USA.

British Steel has spent about £3 billion on new plant during the last 5 years, but still generates the lowest value added per employee of all world steel producers. Output in British Steel is 131 tonnes per man per year. In Germany it is 225, in the USA 274, and in Japan 372. Japanese car plants produce 18 cars per man per year; British Leyland averages 5.6.

Productivity is a Board responsibility. Performance and productivity are directly related. Productivity, performance and the cash generated quite naturally delimit how much can be invested in the further cycle to improve productivity, performance and cash generated.

Quite apart from international comparisons, the absolute performance of UK companies severely curtails opportunity for adventurous investment in the future. The Bank of England has calculated that the real rate of pre-tax return on capital in the UK (non-North Sea) has fallen from 11.5 per cent in 1963 to under 5 per cent in the first half of 1980. Boards are having to divest and retrench for survival. They would have to do so, even without the pressure of a recession.

At least some of the pressures on the Board are beyond its power to influence, individually.

The single company can do nothing about the levels of bank interest, money supply or exchange rate which combine to describe, in large part, the rate of inflation which it will have to live with. Destructive, induced inflation is not a new phenomenon; it was excessive production of paper money that led to the fall of the Sung dynasty in AD 1278. Even the resultant levels of wage and salary increases which it will therefore have to concede will be only partly in its power to influence, individually.

But in combination with like Boards, it does have potential to influence more than one of these factors through its industry associations and spokesbodies. The Board does carry an element of responsibility to encourage its own industry 'power groups' to do what they can to resist unreasonable pressures from the other power groups of government and trade unions.

When it fails to do so, both its company and its industry can be weakened. For long one of the most visible conflicts of attrition has been fought out in Fleet Street, and related corners of the printing industry. It cannot be coincidental that when the conflict is at its toughest, the British Printing Industries Federation is, internally, at its weakest.

Alien practice and participation

Alien practice

The company law directives of the EEC stem from provisions in the Treaty of Rome, which were intended to facilitate the freedom of establishment of companies within the EEC and to protect the interests of members and third parties.

Like any other bureaucracy, the EEC machine will go on extending its interpretation of this 'brief', and its consequent generation of directives, until such time as the men who control the machine decide to switch it off.

There are currently four such directives on the EEC statute book, with several more in draft. The parliaments of member countries are bound to enact the adopted directives within their local legislation, against a timetable established by the Europarliament.

The later directives cause more debate, wider differences of opinion, or more direct opposition than the earlier. The longer the Eurolegislators are left to deliberate, the more detailed their drafts will become, and the more disagreement will inevitably arise.

The First Directive related to publication by each company of its Memorandum, Articles, balance sheet and profit and loss accounts, and required registration data to be recorded on the company's letterhead. It added that a company has a liability to third parties, even if the acts of the Directors which created the liabilities were ultra vires. No local problems arose, and all EEC countries have implemented the directive in localised formats.

The Second Directive related to details of formation of 'public' limited companies, and again caused little conflict. The UK Companies Act of 1980 has covered these requirements (plus a variety of other matters).

The Third Directive relates to internal 'asset' mergers between public companies within the same Group, when the acquired company is dissolved without liquidation. It does not apply to 'share' mergers, which are the kind which occur most frequently in the UK.

The Fourth Directive relates to information to be contained in company accounts, and seeks to make all accounts in the

EEC comparable within three categories of company, defined by size.

The top category is required to provide the most information, and covers organisations which exceed two of the three criteria of:

- turnover of £5 million;
- net assets of £2.5 million;
- 250 employees.

The low size limits applied to this largest category illustrate that company units in the EEC countries are commonly smaller than in the UK. (The success of many of these small European companies in worldwide markets suggests that much could be achieved by their internationally less active British equivalents, given a strengthening of marketing experience in the UK Boardrooms, and a rewriting of their international objectives.)

The middle category covers all public companies which do not meet two of the above criteria, plus all private companies not in the top or bottom categories.

The bottom category covers private companies which do not exceed two of the following criteria:

- turnover of £1.3 million;
- net assets of £650 thousand;
- 50 employees.

While it is acknowledged in the consultative document that special creditors, such as banks, could well require a higher level of information than the very light contents defined as necessary from the smaller categories, it is already clear that there will be considerable disagreement about the proposals overall.

Leaving aside the Fifth Directive for the moment, we have also the Sixth Directive, covering prospectuses for a stock exchange quotation. Adopted by the Europarliament, and unlikely to cause problems in the UK.

The Seventh Directive requires consolidated accounts for all undertakings which are managed on a unified basis by a dominant undertaking, regardless of whether or not there is direct control through shareholding. It would be applied to partnerships and Groups where there is no clear parent, and would mean changes in the UK, which currently only accepts a greater than 50 per cent shareholding as the criterion for control.

The Eighth Directive requires rigid educational standards for auditors, and other details which have already caused controversy, for example, within the House of Lords Select Committee considering it.

Further tentative draft proposals cover, to choose a few examples: unit trusts; winding up of solvent companies, goods sold subject to reservation of title; takeovers; 'scissions' (the reverse of the Third Directive); accounts for insurance companies and banks (not covered in the Fourth Directive); international mergers.

And, six years after a first text was submitted to the EEC Council, the draft for a European company statute is still moving from office to office.

But back to the Fifth Directive, on which the previous relatively passive acceptance of the main contents of EEC company legislation has been abruptly halted, largely on the initiative of the British Conservative Members of the Europarliament.

The first draft of the Fifth Directive was prepared by a former German trade union leader in 1972. By 1978, and after a series of to-ings and fro-ings between the various parts of the EEC machine, the proposals for two-tier Boards, with worker and union Directors on the 'upper' supervisory tier, had come to resemble the current German system (see Appendix II). After rejection of those proposals by the Legal Affairs Committee, and the drafting of alternative proposals, it now seems probable that the final directive, when it eventually appears, will allow UK companies to choose either a two-tier or a unitary style of Board, with employee representation either on the 'upper' supervisory tier, or within an advisory body or 'works council', closely linked to the Board but separate from it.

The danger in adopting alien practice without dissecting every detail of its local suitability, and rejecting whatever is considered harmful or irrelevant, is that the pressure to adopt increasingly alien practice would itself increase. Had the UK accepted freely the requirements of the original draft Fifth Directive, how long would have passed before the UK, and other EEC countries, would have been required to enact the kind of profit sharing or equity sharing which is now being pressed for adoption in Scandinavia?

Certainly the more extreme, and largely political, proposals current in Denmark and Sweden would prove unpalatable in many parts of the EEC, but they have already been publicly aired with a degree of force in Germany, Holland and the UK.

Consider the Swedish proposals of the Meidner Plan, which are echoed in Danish trade union proposals. These would allow for shares to be allocated progressively out of profits, a percentage of which would be placed in a fund under trade union control. The allocation would build up until a controlling percentage of the equity had been achieved. An extraordinary mixture of extreme socialism and cold capitalism, which would put the control of capitalism in the hands of its natural 'adversary'.

Consider also the Swedish legislation of 1977 for employee participation in decision making. An official Swedish publication states that this law 'implies the birth of a new order. Labour and Capital are to be regarded as equals where the right of decision-making is concerned'. The thesis that labour equals capital defies all logic. The assumption that Boards and company management represent capital also defies both logic and existing law.

The majority report of the Bullock Committee of Inquiry on Industrial Democracy (a British attempt to produce proposals for employee participation, which floundered largely because it was given terms of reference which begged the question to be considered) also made the same mistake of confusing capital with the management of companies. It wrote about 'putting the relationship between capital and labour on to a new basis which will involve not just management but the whole work-force in sharing responsibility for the success and profitability of the enterprise'.

But the content and intent of the law regarding companies is that capital, or shareholding, is separated from management. The Board does not represent capital; it represents the company. It can only effectively control the company if its membership is confined to those who have the experience, knowledge, skill and commitment to actually contribute to the company's survival and eventual prosperity.

The political nature of developments in Sweden, which sadly provides example for politically motivated organisations in other countries, including the UK, is illustrated by the fact that its legislation for worker Directors, like its equivalent in Denmark, does not allow the worker Directors to participate in Boardroom discussion on any questions of industrial unrest, strikes or similar – the very questions on which they might be expected to have some specialist expertise or contribution to make to the Board's decisions.

Certainly the Swedes and the Danes have a facility for stretching logic beyond its elastic limits when it comes to political participation, for example in other recent legislation which requires the Board to negotiate almost every major question with the unions in advance of decision. This is not participation: it is abdication.

The employee in the UK already has a steadily increasing stake in capital, albeit indirect. The holdings of pension funds, insurance companies and other institutions take an additional 2 per cent each year of the equity of quoted companies, and currently hold close to 70 per cent of the total. This does not provide the employee with seats on any Boards, but nor should this, or any other criterion, provide such seats, except the criterion of an ability to contribute to Board performance.

Through all debate on the question of participation, which will lie heavy on Boards and their spokesbodies during the coming years, it is essential that the pressures for improved company performance and for political advantage be kept clinically separate. It might be noted as passing encouragement that pressure for a politically motivated power sharing does not arise in either the US or Japan, two countries which well illustrate a collective understanding, from shopfloor to Boardroom, about the overriding importance of corporate performance.

Subsequent chapters examine the separate questions of two-tier Boards, and employee or union Directors, and dismiss them as unhelpful in a UK context.

Participation

The question of participation must not be dismissed. The Board, for as long as it retains the freedom to decide what is good for its company, must establish and refine forms of employee involvement which will increase employee satisfaction, and thus improve employee morale, cooperation and productivity.

Employees want:

- to be informed;
- to be involved wherever they can sensibly contribute;
- to be able to have their grievances readily reviewed, and
- to be sure that they are not being overridden roughshod.

Boards may consider aiding participation by:

(a) schemes for profit sharing among all or some of the employees, and/or

(b) schemes for allocating shares among employees.

The problem with (a) is that motivation becomes too remote when the scheme is extended beyond top managers and Directors. The return to other employees is best left in the form of fatter wage packets. The problem with (b) is that most employees work in subsidiaries, or private independent companies which have restrictions on share transfer. The individual performance of a subsidiary may differ greatly from the performance of the parent, whose shares are allocated, and again the motivation and interest become too remote.

On the other hand Boards must:

establish and maintain effective channels for two-way communication and consultation at all levels to the shopfloor.

Communication covers details of people and organisation; progress made by the company; policy made by the Board. It is to enable innovative comment, or complaint, to pass smoothly and certainly upwards, and facts and judgements to pass clearly downwards. Consultation covers problems or projects. It is intended to eliminate misunderstanding; to achieve an acceptance of changes proposed; to obtain the contribution of employees, where they have one to make; thereby to achieve improved performance. Employees must know they are genuinely involved, that they are an integral part of the company and are viewed as such by the Board, and that their prosperity depends on the prosperity of the whole. Without involvement there can be no real commitment. Without commitment there can be little chance of adequate performance.

If he works for you, you work for him.

JAPANESE PROVERB

Each company has a unique structure or character. Each needs to adapt its participation mechanism to that structure and character. One firm guideline is that the groupings formed for communication and consultation should parallel the structure of the company. There should be a 'works council', by any better name, at holding board level, outside of that board but containing some of its Directors; one in each division; one in each subsidiary. The councils should be identified with the business units with which the members themselves identify. Composition of the councils must be decided by each level, with the Board keeping an eye over the whole to see that they do this with sense and sensitivity. About half line and functional management, about half employees, including, where relevant, the union representative – though this is one forum which the union representative must not be allowed to dominate. Each council should contain one representative of management who is able to take on-the-spot decisions on straightforward questions, which almost inevitably means the unit's Chief Executive.

The Board which does not know how or where to begin should have an initial talk with the Industrial Society, and thence continue with or without their further assistance. There is already a considerable body of experience on participation schemes within the UK. Companies ranging from ICI at one extreme, and a host of unsophisticated small companies at the other, have had successful participation schemes for years, even decades. The Industrial Society, a combined management/union organisation, has helped introduce many.

A number of companies shelved their tentative thinking about participation after the irrelevancies of the Bullock Inquiry. Resolve to reopen the subject, as a Board priority, can be stiffened by the knowledge that participation in Europe works well between unions, employees and managements, at operational levels. They all tend to ignore the existence of the more political supervisory board level. Employees are interested in their persons, not in politics, and they will help establish businesslike schemes, given the chance. So give them the chance. Let the Board, at all levels, work out the schemes and the council compositions, together with the employees.

Do not forget the representation of the 'middle level'. Detailed creativity in a company, as contrasted with broader strategic innovation, emanates largely from the specialist or middle-manager level, which is sandwiched, and squeezed, between the shopfloor and the Boardroom. The Japanese have long recognised this in their painfully slow, but thoroughly effective, 'ringi' system of consultation.

The only effective participation scheme is one which covers all levels equally, as a glove covers all the fingers.

Customer and community

Consumerism

Consumerism remains more restrained in the UK and Europe than in the US, and still shows none of the wilder American extremes. There is little sign of any enthusiasm for putting consumer representatives onto Boards. The unexciting experience of nationalised industry Boards, which experimented with such representatives, suggests that others will not be in a hurry to try the same.

A consumer has the natural objective of obtaining as much as possible for as little as possible, with the tightest strings attaching. Boards, in contrast, have to be free to make up their own minds how to obtain a sufficient number of customers, at a sufficient price, to a sufficient but not triple-plated specification, at acceptable cost. (All, coincidentally, the most confidential of competitive business data.) The role of lobbying for improved service, specification or price is thus best placed outside of the Board, in a separate consumers' consultative committee if the Board finds this helpful. And then only in the case of nationalised industries, or other corporations which luxuriate in monopoly or near-monopoly situations where normal market pressures do not automatically apply.

For the rest, there is surely adequate concerted external pressure on companies from national and EEC bodies such as Consumers in the European Community Group (UK), which is an umbrella organisation coordinating the research and representations of the main UK organisations interested in UK consumer affairs and EEC policies – including the Consumers' Association, Good Housekeeping Institute, National Consumer Council, National Consumer Protection Council, National Council of Women, and 16 other like organisations – as well as the European bodies CCC, ECOSOC, BEUC, EUROCOOP and COFACE.

The EEC is seeking to establish a range of rules and regulations regarding how to service the customer, some helpful, some less so, but all amenable to reasonable debate. The British Consumer Affairs Minister did comment that some of these moves are 'positively harmful' because they inhibited action by national governments, but the comment seems little justified in view of the broadly useful steps taken to date. The First Consumer Action Programme of the EEC was based on most sensible principles:

- elimination of health or safety hazards;
- protection against injury from defective products or services;
- control of additives to foodstuffs and prevention of contamination from packaging;
- specific rules for machinery and electrical products, e.g. type approval;
- harmonised procedures within the EEC for new products which could be harmful to health or safety.

The Second Programme 1980–85 will centre on:

- harmonisation of laws to enable free movement of products;
- further health and safety details, e.g. re motor vehicle components and other manufactured products;

- further monitoring of additives, as well as of labelling and misleading or unfair advertising;
- further rules regarding cosmetics;
- inflammability of textiles;
- safety of toys;
- home accident surveillance;
- further safeguards re pharmaceuticals (e.g. for veterinary use) and dangerous substances;
- after-sales service, including regulations about guarantee periods and replacement parts;
- the quality of certain services, including public services.

It would be difficult to argue against the value of a well-marshalled review of all these subjects, or against the need for a range of common standards within the EEC trading boundaries, though there are clearly far more semi-official bodies involved than are necessary. Some resistance is developing on the question of what it costs the manufacturer to take account of the new rules, and all costs are reflected inevitably in the price to the consumer. In the USA, where consumerism began and where it has become unreasonably noisy, a strong backlash to the consumer movement is growing, based largely on the question of resulting cost and price increases. Four factors affect this question more heavily in the US than they are ever likely to do in Europe and the UK:

- the frequency of 'class' actions, a phenomenon almost unknown in Europe and the UK;
- the frequent assessment and exaggeration of damages by a US jury, rather than by a judge, as in the UK;
- the relating of damages to be paid to the subjective extent of the 'misdeed' by the company, not to any objective assessment of the harm actually incurred;
- the fact that US lawyers commonly work on a 'contingency fee' basis, taking as much as 30 per cent of a successful settlement.

In the UK, complaint about the pressure on costs is little justified. There have been rumbles from the Commercial Legislation Monitoring Group, which consists of 18 major organisations such as Unilever, Imperial Group, Marks & Spencer and the CBI. The CBI has gone on record that in certain cases 'already costs outweigh the benefits to consumers'. But consider the facts. An Economist Intelligence Unit study concluded that these additional costs, in their entirety, and including the costs of price controls (now abolished) and restrictive trade practices legislation, averaged only one penny in every £10 of retail sales, plus possibly an additional 50 per cent of this for enforcement. By any standard a small and acceptable fraction – and surely acceptable at several times this fraction, given that these costs are shared equally by all manufacturers in the same businesses and can be passed on equally, without the slightest chance of the consumer noticing. There would be no shift in competitive advantage or disadvantage, which is what the Board has to worry about when composing its marketing strategies.

The loudest rumblings against the cost of consumer protection relate to those which would arise from the draft EEC directive on product liability. This seeks to place liability for damage caused by defective products directly on the manufacturer, irrespective of whether or not the manufacturer is considered to have been negligent.

The expensive chain of claim and counter-claim back from retailer to manufacturer would be eliminated, and those able to receive compensation would be extended, properly, to cover the person actually suffering the damage, not just the original purchaser.

The British Conservative government has stated that it accepts industry's argument that a 'state of the art' defence should be allowed. This defence means that if a defect in a new product could not reasonably have been foreseen, the manufacturer is not liable for any damage caused by the product. This stand would nullify the proposed effect of a very sensible EEC directive. Had this been the situation in the Thalidomide case, half of the victims would not have received compensation. The British government's view is misguided. Several European countries already provide protection equivalent to that proposed in the directive.

When deciding the stand each Board will take in this specific debate, Directors can usefully take into account the opinion of one of the largest insurance companies that, even if a company's product liability insurance premium has to double to cover this new risk, the cost will only increase from about 0.01 per cent of turnover to 0.02 per cent. Hardly worth another sentence when inflation is bouncing about in double figures on the left-hand side of the decimal point.

A company goes out of business if customers stop buying its products, even if it loses only a quarter or a third of its customers. They may choose to stop buying for a range of reasons, from danger, to price, service, fashion or nationalism. The Board's responsibility is to the company, to ensure that the products are such that the customer goes on buying them. It has few direct responsibilities to the customer, beyond using its best endeavours to ensure that the products are safe, and properly described and advertised. With industrial goods there is little problem; description of goods, performance and specification are laid down in a detailed contract. With consumer goods the borderline between commercial sense in satisfying the customer and legal responsibility in protecting the customer is getting blurred.

> *If directors were doing their jobs properly, consumer organisations would not exist. Tough, but it is true.*
>
> MISS EIRLYS ROBERTS, CBE

The consumer movement grew up because companies were not exercising enough 'commercial sense'. The movement now has a momentum of its own, and legal requirements will go beyond 'commercial sense', seen from a company's viewpoint alone. No manufacturer would, without legislation, volunteer the information on his jar of face cream that the contents are 63 per cent water.

Because manufacturers became lax in keeping the customer sensibly informed, they are now certain to have to contend with a whole new bundle of regulations and legislation. Indeed, the point has been reached where Directors can scarcely be blamed for taking few new initiatives of their own until told what to do by such detailed legislation. Legislation is necessary. Codes do not work. The AMDEA Code on servicing for domestic electrical equipment has not improved the level of service afforded to the customer.

There is a brighter side. While industry as a whole characteristically abhors legislation of any kind, the producer can be aided by a clear statement of responsibilities which affect all producers in his field, equally. The wise Board will contribute fully to the battle to format statements of responsibilities to the customer, so that these do come to lie at a sensible mid-point between the extreme 'interests' of the customer and the producer.

In the long run, what is good for the customer will be good for the most effective of the competing producers.

The Competition Act, 1980

Of greater potential concern to the UK Board are the possible effects of the 1980 Competition Act. This gives wide-ranging powers to the Office of Fair Trading, the width of the powers stemming largely from the haziness of their definition.

Though the Conservative government which introduced it proclaims a policy of non-intervention in industry, this Act appears to achieve the very opposite. The CBI opposed it, but too mildly; perhaps out of politeness to a new and hopefully friendly government still finding its feet; perhaps out of eagerness to see the death of the Price Commission, which was also accomplished by the Act.

Among its provisions the Act empowers the Director-General of Fair Trading to investigate anti-competitive practices, the definition of which covers any course of conduct which has the effect of 'restricting, preventing or distorting competition'. The company concerned need not be a dominant supplier, nor need there be any advance evidence of collusion of any kind.

If he concludes in his judgement that a practice investigated is in fact anti-competitive, the Director-General can either request and accept undertakings from the company concerned that it will discontinue the practice, or can refer the matter to the Monopolies and Mergers Commission. In the latter case the MMC has six months in which to report, and the Secretary of State for Trade must publish the report. He can make an order prohibiting the company from engaging in the practice, or can instruct the Director-General to seek undertakings to the same effect.

The government which enacted the legislation has stated

that it anticipates about 20–30 investigations a year, and indicated during the committee stage of the Bill that the type of practices which might be investigated include:

- discriminatory pricing discounts;
- predatory pricing – use of selective cuts to inhibit new competition;
- minimum advertised prices;
- refusal to supply cut-price retailers;
- refusal to supply new retailers in a specific area;
- refusal to supply, except to a limited number of retailers who undertake to pay a higher price for exclusivity;
- exclusive dealing – where two or more parties accept restrictions on the supply and sale of goods or services;
- supply to certain categories of retailer;
- tie-in sales – the sale of one product being linked to another;
- rental-only contracts;
- loyalty rebates – where rebates are given for restricting sales of competitive products.

While the government accepted that many of these practices are not always against the public interest, the Director-General may still investigate any one or more of them, in any company he chooses, subject only to the veto of the Trade Secretary. The Trade Secretary himself can ask the MMC to open an investigation, including, for the first time, into a nationalised industry. The first report on an investigation into British Rail has already been published.

At best the Act avoids the pitfalls of US anti-trust laws, under which each potential breach is battled through the courts at huge cost to both corporations and taxpayers. At worst it brings sharply to mind that the political colour of governments, Trade Secretaries or even Directors-General can all change with time.

The Restrictive Trade Practices Act, 1976

In the early 1970s a number of cases were brought against contracting companies in the mechanical and electrical services fields for their collusive tendering in the 1960s, a process whereby the bidders for a contract came together covertly to decide which of them would win the particular tender at what price – the others then agreeing to increase their own bids well above that figure.

Similar collusion had been detected in the fields of ready-mixed concrete, road surfacing materials, and telephone cables – also companies selling mainly to public authorities which had major construction projects to complete. The net result was that the public authorities, which in the final analysis means the general public, ended up paying inflated prices to these subcontractors.

The practice was against the existing civil law, hence the court actions. It was against the public interest. And it was commercially inept. When the companies were instructed by the courts to desist, they found that after a number of years of surviving on artificial prices they were no longer able to build up a commercially competitive tender. It was all a bit like the situation of the ageing Afghans who purchased hormones from the pharmaceuticals company in which the writer first cut his commercial teeth. True, these artificial aids kept them in the condition to which they were accustomed for as long as the aids were available. But once deprived of them, the gentlemen discovered that they had chemically emasculated themselves, irreversibly.

Many of the largest UK contractors began to run into losses. Uncertainty led to price cutting, which led them into deeper losses. It took some clear thinking, and relentless Board monitoring, to restore a measure of commercial sense.

Yet although the practice was illegal, against the public interest and demonstrably destructive in the long term, the new Restrictive Trade Practices Act of 1976, which was introduced to protect the customer and the community, did not make the practice a criminal offence (except where the colluding parties had already been ordered by the court to desist).

It is a criminal offence in Canada, Australia, Germany and the US, and is prohibited with greater or lesser severity in most other parts of Europe. In Germany in 1975 fines totalling £10 million were imposed on a large number of construction companies, and on nearly 500 individual managers, who had been involved in the practice.

A mid-1980 Consultative Document from the Department of Trade has now recommended that the practice be branded as criminal in the UK also, to carry unlimited fines and up to two years in prison. Boards beware.

Of the many forms of corrupt practice, this one is significantly different. Unlike old-fashioned bribery of officials, it excludes the customer.

The community

The CBI stated in 1973 that '. . . a company, like a natural person, must be recognised as having functions, duties and moral obligations that go beyond the pursuit of profit and the specific requirements of legislation'. But the company is not like a natural person. It is created, described and confined by specific legislation. It is created for a specific purpose. Its relationship with its environment in achieving that purpose is similarly defined by legislation, such as the Acts concerning health and safety, pollution, taxation and employment, which are intended to ensure that it does not abuse its community, in the widest sense of the word.

The Companies Acts of 1948, 1967, 1976 and 1980 also define a range of limitations on corporate behaviour, which have the same objective. The Act of 1980 lists 135 offences, ranging from minor breaches which lead to minor fines, to major offences which can place an individual Director in prison for several years.

The company must comply with all laws which affect all similar companies. It cannot fancy out ways of being more good. It cannot develop the qualities of a natural person, such as goodness and charity.

Companies are not created to be charitable to their external community. They are created to do business, and through that process to create wealth for

- their own internal community of employees;
- the public-representing institutions, and individuals, which own shares in them;
- the taxman, and through him the community at large. He has the largest stake of all.

The Board has quite enough to do attending to those responsibilities. It is the role of governments to attend to the community.

4   *Types of Board*

All Boards

The control of a company is separated by law from the ownership of its shares. The rights of the shareholders are few in number, but potentially powerful if resolutely exercised. They include the rights:

- to ensure that the company is properly administered;
- to elect or remove the Directors;
- to receive information in accordance with the Companies Acts;
- to appoint the auditors;
- to approve the accounts;

Given a 75 per cent majority:

- to alter the Articles and redefine the powers of the Directors.

In extreme circumstances:

- to request the Department of Trade to investigate the company;
- to take legal action against the Directors;
- to petition for a winding-up of the company.

The fiduciary and contractual relationships of all the Directors are to the company, not to the shareholders. They operate in accordance with the powers and responsibilities defined in the company's Articles, and in the Companies Acts, and they exercise them collectively, not individually, within the Boardroom.

Within these broad definitions, the Board may determine what types and limits of action and decision it will reserve to itself, and what it will delegate to whom, always bearing in mind that no functions or powers can be delegated without express provision in the Articles that this may be done. No Managing Director can be appointed without similar provision.

The company will change over the years by size and markets, and by structure and strength, and the Board's priority of responsibilities will need to change in step. At any stage of development the Board, as the governing body, will not be able to control the company without retaining to itself the responsibility:

- to select or remove individual Directors, alter their mix, and compose the Board as a productive entity;
- to select or replace the Chairman of the Board;
- to select or remove the Managing Director/Chief Executive;
- to define the limits of authority of the Chief Executive in terms of expenditure, appointments, businesses, contracts and functions. To define similar limits of authority for other Directors and top managers, or alternatively to approve those defined by the Chief Executive. To approve their detailed job descriptions and lists of routine duties. (Without clear definition of precisely what is delegated and what is expected, there can be little blame attaching to subsequent inaction.) In particular, to describe what is required from each non-executive Director, in terms of time and type of contribution expected;
- to approve the appointment or removal of top managers immediately below the Board. It is sensible policy at all levels in the company to ensure that appointments or dismissals are referred, for prior approval, one notch above the man's immediate superior;
- to define or approve similar limits of authority for subsidiary companies, and for their senior executives;
- to compile and communicate a set of company policies covering:
    fundamental beliefs about style of operation, if any
    personnel policies

external and internal relations, communication and
participation

market sectors and businesses

required return on capital (ROC) and related performance standards

acquisition, divestment, diversification and organic
growth policies

planning and budgeting procedures;

- to review the business alternatives open to the company
on an ongoing basis, and arrange that meaningful plans
are produced at all levels, covering the longest realistic
time scales. For large companies, this may be twenty
years at corporate level, but only three years at subsidiary level. With smaller companies, quantitative planning is difficult to stretch beyond about three years, but
qualitative planning needs to look further ahead. Out of
which process comes the sacred one-year budget;

- and through this process, to determine the total
resources of the company, both actual and potential, in
men, money, methods and market position. To allocate
these by unit and time scale, defining closely what
returns, and when, these resources are required to
generate;

- to advise management in the compilation of plans and
strategies, and to assist, where this would be helpful, in
their implementation. If executive and non-executive
Directors are truly experienced in business operations,
they are sure to have some knowledge or opinions which
can be useful to managers outside of the Boardroom.
Particularly in smaller or subsidiary companies;

- to structure and organise the company as a whole, determining that units and key individuals can interrelate
productively, that the good ones can grow without
hindrance, and that the machinery of the company
'works';

- to describe and communicate how and what it will communicate. To map out the mechanism for internal
liaison, upwards, downwards and sideways between
units;

- to describe a similar mechanism for external communication, determining which Directors will be responsible for each category of liaison. The external world includes customers, suppliers, lenders, the media, government bodies, and sometimes the local community – not just actual or potential shareholders and city analysts;

– to develop a mechanism for employee participation at all levels, to the extent, and in the style, which both the Board and the employees agree is most suitable to the company. To determine from time to time that participation is real, alive, and treated as an asset, not a nuisance. As recorded in the Companies Act of 1980, the Board is responsible for taking account of the interests of the employees, within the overriding interests of the company as a whole. Without effective working mechanisms for participation and communication, the Board may never be able to discover what those interests really are, beyond the always obvious questions of pay and rations;

– to define how the Board itself will operate, what routines it will adopt, what it will look at and decide monthly, quarterly and annually. To determine in careful detail how, and with what data, it will monitor the performance of management and the financial progress of the company;

– to monitor management performance against both one-year budgets and longer-term plan figures. If performance against budgets is widely astray, there may be something wrong with management. If performance against the plan progression is widely astray, there may be something wrong with the policies or strategies on which the Board has relied;

– to close, and keep closed, the loop of analysis, evaluation, decision, planning, implementation, monitoring, adapting, monitoring. . . . One of the strongest arguments in favour of the unitary Board system is that the company's top decision point in this continuous process lies within the loop, not outside of nor tangential to it;

– to monitor its own performance as a Board, at least annually. To place an item on the agenda at which each of the Directors really feels that his contribution is in the spotlight, including the Chairman and each of the non-executives. If each has contributed with energy and value, he will feel no discomfort. The Board represents the most important of the company's investments. The performance of that investment should be as closely reviewed as the returns on any other expenditure.

Holding Boards

The Holding Board (or 'Main' or 'Group' Board,) is to its subsidiaries as the independent company is to its individual businesses. They both decide what resources they will allocate to each of the activities for which they are responsible; determine what returns they require from each; appoint managers to operate each; decide how they will monitor each; then control the corporate whole by monitoring the returns which the managers generate from those resources.

The Holding Board's first decision is whether the subsidiaries are to operate as real companies. If so, the subsidiaries will need real Boards of their own, operating freely within a set of limits of authority. If not, the Holding Board's management responsibilities become very great, and the responsibilities of the managers, or the let's-pretend Directors of the subsidiaries, become very much less. The Holding Board cannot 'have it both ways'.

There is no rule of thumb applicable to all Groups at all stages of growth which can describe when centralisation of responsibility and control will be more effective than decentralisation; which is one reason why some Groups are observed to organise and reorganise periodically from one extreme to the other, apparently willy-nilly. Nor is there any rule which suggests that the Holding Board must handle each of its subsidiaries in the same way. Different units at different stages of growth, or with different problems or opportunities, can be controlled differently. The Board can handle one at arm's length, and then rootle into the smallest details of another, at the same Board meeting.

The best guideline is that the Board should select for its

Chief Executive a man who is by nature primarily people-oriented, rather than primarily figures or machinery-oriented; who can readily accept that his main role is to engage people for positions below him who are good enough to operate entirely without him. Many Chief Executives cannot 'stand back' from their position to this extent, or will not take the risk which this might seem to involve. But only this will enable the Board to push authority downwards, with any confidence. Without confidence, it has to retain a heavily centralised structure and control.

As the Group's top manager, the Holding Board has a number of responsibilities, either in law or in practice, which interface or overlap with those of management below it. The Board has to describe to management where it will interface, and where it should choose to overlap. In setting these boundaries it must be ready, and be seen to be ready, to take advice from management as to where a proposed interface should be an overlap, or, more likely, where management feels the opposite should be preferred. The Board will make its own decisions, but will acquire credit and credibility by at least seeming to share this kind of decision. When there is any doubt, the Board should settle for a closer, rather than remoter, involvement. Subsequent complaint from management that the Board 'interferes' too much may be valid. Or it may signal that management has something to hide. Or that it has nothing of significance to expose.

During the 1960s and 1970s fashion yo-yoed between centralisation and decentralisation rather as the contemporary hem-line rose and fell, to some extent in accordance with what the haute consulting houses were promoting that season. Any reader who has walked into the shambles which often followed one of those freshly-introduced 'broad strategic concepts' of centralisation or decentralisation (it matters not a jot which of the two) will know that the concept seldom got down to looking at how things would actually have to work in detail in areas a notch or two below the Holding Board.

The fault for the futility of many of these expensive manipulations did not lie wholly with the haute consulting houses. Too often the Board which commissioned and briefed them for the reorganisation project had been well bitten by the bug of change, but had not known its company well enough to know where it really needed to scratch.

Structural change demands close understanding of how the smallest parts of the company's businesses are pursued and completed; where the company is strong, and how in practice it is weak; which managers are effective and which are misplaced. Structures only work if the theoretical ideal is first calculated clinically, and is then adapted a little to suit the peculiarities of those markets and managers judged to be most valuable to the company.

The Board's role in determining the optimum structure becomes more onerous as the Group diversifies. A natural objective in the plans of most Holding Boards is steadily to increase both the size and the variety of their businesses, at least partly as a defence mechanism to dissuade predators which might find 'size' quite easy to swallow, but 'diversity' more difficult to digest.

Growing diversity itself forces the Holding Board to push large portions of policy making down line, while tightening the machinery for central monitoring. The reality and effectiveness with which the Holding Board then keeps control of its total business becomes dependent, firstly, on the quality of the reporting and monitoring system and, secondly, on the quality of the chain of individuals linking that Board through to the lowest operating levels.

While it is always partly true that 'management is all about people', this is always entirely true in relation to how, and how well, the Holding Board manages its Group.

Private companies

The roles and responsibilities of public and private company main Boards differ only in secondary detail. On the one hand, the public company has more onerous external communication commitments. It has to satisfy the enquiries of analysts, brokers, journalists and corporate shareholders. It is under greater pressure to preserve an appearance of unity and calm within the Boardroom, as a demonstration of its ability to handle its affairs smoothly.

On the other hand, the private company restricts the number of its members, restricts the transfer of its shares, and has to submit annual statements that it has done so. And there the theoretical differences end.

The Companies Act of 1948 defined the private company by reference to these restrictions, and left public companies as the undefined residue. The Act of 1980 has reversed this situation by defining the public company, now to be designated 'public limited company', or plc, and leaving a residue comprising the private companies.

In round figures, there are over 600,000 registered private companies in the UK, ranging from man-and-wife teams to major international enterprises. There are about 16,000 public companies, of which 2,800 are listed on the London Stock Exchange.

There are more domestic, or British registered, listed companies on the London Stock Exchange than there are domestic listed companies in all the other exchanges in the countries of the EEC put together. Brussels has 231, Copenhagen 224, Paris 595, the combined German exchanges 458, Milan 138, Luxembourg 69, and Amsterdam 216. (Totals for Eire are included with the UK domestic figure, in accordance with long-standing practice, and number just under 100.)

British public companies are on average larger than equivalents in Europe. It may also be surprising that the average size of factory or production unit in the UK is larger than the average in any other country, including Germany, Japan, or even the US.

The argument has been raised that the Europeans outperform the British because of the predominance of small, and smaller private, companies in Europe. This has stimulated a spasm or two of public debate on the need to create more small private companies in the UK, as well as some activity by government and a handful of large corporations to provide assistance to such companies.

The facts do not support the argument that 'small is beautiful' in the UK, at least in terms of profitability. The comparative data available (see Appendix III) show that private UK companies perform less well than public UK companies, generating a much lower rate of profit, despite a faster rate of growth in turnover and a higher pro rata level of investment.

There are a number of qualitative factors which contribute to the lesser performance of the small private company in the UK, whether it be compared with local public companies, or with European companies as a whole. These are subject to honourable exceptions, but they will strike several chords with those who are experienced in small company affairs. Broadly:

- 'small' in the UK normally means 'private'. UK private companies are able to keep very private indeed, and their filed returns, while meeting the law's requirements, still manage to describe very little;
- small private companies in Europe operate commonly to the same, or similar, professional standards as large local companies. They do not correlate size with sophistication. The management sophistication of a company employing 100 people in Denmark would stagger most British executives, including those in UK public companies;
- the skilled European executive will work readily in a smaller local company which pays him well and gives him the kinds of challenge and role he likes to undertake. The equivalent British executive knows that it normally damages his curriculum vitae to move 'down' from a larger into a smaller company, and the small UK company has much difficulty in attracting good staff. And then in keeping them; the head hunters know that most UK executives can be attracted to join a larger company;
- the smaller UK company therefore lacks expertise, either because some of its key people are lightweight, or because it has gaps in the skills employed. It has considerable need for external doses of expertise, in the form of traditional consultancy, or for internal professional support for its managers in the form of 'active' non-executive Directors. But the smaller UK company commonly considers both categories of support to be close to parasitic, and seldom uses either, however great the

demonstrable need. Better the 'parasitic' consultant than the saprophytic receiver;

- as a consequence, management and accounting techniques are clumsy, reporting is primitive, monitoring is hit-and-miss, resources are often unproductive, planning is rudimentary or absent;
- the few dominant shareholders, who are normally also the dominant Directors, even in large private companies where their combined stakes represent a minority, find it difficult to divorce shareholding from directorship – as the law requires them to do. Too often 'private' still means 'personal', despite the fact that the company is registered under national legislation;
- in the UK private company, often also when they are large, the Board is commonly composed of one or two families and their nominees, plus perhaps a sprinkling of retired executives and a few chums. The power struggles in the Boardroom, in the absence of truly professional and independent outside non-executives, can come to resemble the family feuds once common in the 'Old West', and still common on the North-West Frontier – conflicts quite irrelevant to the business in hand;
- with the main shareholders already inside the Board, and the main lenders almost always passive till the very moment the company is sick unto death, there is no source of external pressure to improve Board composition and company performance. There is no external pressure for change, no inclination to engage external expertise to assist with change, and often no internal recognition of the need for change. Small UK companies consistently run into trouble, or go into liquidation, when they grow through a 'change step' without recognising it, and the size of the business overtakes the Board's ability to manage it.

Divisional Boards

A division can be real or apparent. In larger Groups it is normally real. It has Company Limited status, owns all its subsidiaries, operates like its own 'Holding Board' within widely defined limits of authority from its parent, and has a Board of Directors which functions as such, non-executives and all.

Lower down the size scale, a divisional company is often little more than an extra level of management committee, producing less active contribution than its own subsidiaries.

And as the size of the Group decreases, the incidence of the apparent division increases. Subsidiaries with similar characteristics are collected into divisional groupings as much because this looks good in corporate sales literature, as because it might occasionally help to put together into one pot the related problems and opportunities of like-working companies. There is a divisional committee with one of a dozen alternative names, intended to be a forum for airing those related problems and opportunities, and for reaching improved conclusions. It seldom satisfies either intention.

The instinct of territorial protectiveness among subsidiary company executives will always be stronger than the instinct for collective survival, unless the mechanism imposes a collective responsibility by giving the members a level-pegging directorship status.

When the division is apparent, cooperative liaison can become a formality and a frustration. Even the first step of inducing the constituent subsidiary MDs to review each others' figures is seldom worth the hassle, and they will never get round to exposing their innermost concerns.

In a divisional committee the competent manager will use his skills to shield his own unit from scrutiny, drawing attention away from it by adept reference to problems known to exist in other units.

In a Divisional Board, with real teeth and real business objectives, the competent manager, who is now also a Divisional Director, will in contrast use this forum as an enlarged arena in which to exercise his strength. This can only be for the collective good, as the parent company must always be searching for ways of developing the confidence and experience of its best managers, and thus for growing its own future successions.

Good subsidiary company MDs can be vulnerable to dissatisfaction, being at the same time halfway up the management hierarchy, and halfway down to the hard surface

of the shopfloor. They are among the men most easily located
by head hunters out on a 'search'. They may be better than
their boss thinks they are, or better than he wants others to
think they are. So give them a proper divisional Company
Limited pool to swim in, and watch.

Composing Divisional Boards can generate more heartache
or resentment than composing the Holding Board. How many
and which of the subsidiary MDs to include is always a
dilemma, and the selection of the most appropriate functional
specialists can be equally tricky. It is an activity which the
Group Chief Executive alone can seldom carry out to everyone's satisfaction, and is a good reason for requiring the
parent company non-executives, who are accepted as being
'independent', to get to know and evaluate down-line management. In this they can greatly assist the Group Chief Executive, especially when he is suppressing a good man or two for
personal or irrational reasons, and everyone else, including
the independent non-executive, can see this.

The larger the Group, the more instances there are of such
conscious or subconscious suppression. The queen bee will
naturally suppress the development of other queens, and the
Chief Executive will have as much trouble as anyone else in
restraining his own queen bee instincts.

The larger the Group and the wider the division in its
content of subsidiaries, the more vital to the effectiveness of
parental control is the nature of the human linkages from one
level to the next. Where the linkage is through a single-man
chain, Group Chief Executive/Divisional MD/subsidiary
MD/subsidiary executive, each operating as a direct line boss
over subordinates, the parent Board has to work with severely
limited vision. The key people in the chain will each be covering so much other detailed ground that they, too, will 'see' but
a part of the whole.

No man alone is wise enough.

PLAUTUS

More effective is to duplicate or triplicate the linkages, with
the Board at each level requiring one or two of its other
Directors, also, to exercise an active interest in the affairs of
the next level down. The Finance Director or Business

Development Director may be charged in this way with a defined role to review and assist, and indeed quite frequently are. They are sometimes called 'non-executives' when they sit on the next Board down, but cannot truly perform as non-executives because they inevitably represent 'higher authority'.

Much less common, though of great potential value, is the placing of a parent non-executive on each Divisional Board, alongside divisional non-executives who are not on the Holding Board. The mechanism can be repeated downwards onto the Boards of the main subsidiary companies. In any Group, the responsibilities of controlling and assisting, without undue interfering, could be most productively achieved by a planned overlap in Board membership at each adjoining pair of Board levels, including the line boss, a non-executive and a relevant executive Director.

If it is still controversial to recommend that real non-executives should sit on Divisional and subsidiary Boards (and there are very few who do), and if it is quite novel to recommend that some of them should overlap onto two levels of Board, then it must be close to heresy to recommend that the Divisional Board should not be chaired by the Group Chief Executive. But if the line boss of the divisional executives is chairing their Board meetings, then they might well be forgiven for sitting silent from 'Matters Arising' to 'Date of Next Meeting', simply waiting to be told what to do by the man who is their line boss and their Board chairman rolled into one.

The almost universal arrangement whereby the Group Chief Executive does chair the Divisional Boards is not helpful in 'bringing out' the executives, nor in extracting their maximum contribution. Further, it keeps the Group Chief Executive rigidly 'in line' when he could benefit more, and could himself contribute more freely, if he were sitting elsewhere than at the head of the table.

Let a non-executive chair the Divisional Board. Let the Group Chief Executive sit among his colleagues, observing, weighing. No-one is going to deny that he really is the boss just because he does not do all the talking. Heresy this may seem, but it goes to the core of the problem of composing a structure for achieving contribution, and thus performance, in a diverse organisation.

If the Divisional Board, or divisional committee, is to be nothing more than a mechanism for past performance review, then it is not needed at all. If Boards below the Holding Board, because they are weak or small or new, really are to be viewed as management committees, then call them that and avoid the Company Limited status.

But if a grouping of subsidiaries with common markets, technologies or management processes is to benefit from an interchange of ideas, opportunities or men, then it must feel that it is structured and truly empowered to do so. If the parent does want the Divisional Board to take initiatives within defined but uninhibiting limits, to make suggestions, disagree, present better alternatives, evaluate, plan, decide and then implement with the wholehearted commitment of its Directors, then it must create a divisional entity in which the Directors concerned can do all these things with a feeling of excitement, not formality, and with the knowledge that their contributions will not only be visible but will actually be seen.

This will be achieved if the Divisional Board is chaired by a Holding Board non-executive, contains also divisional-level non-executives, plus the Group Chief Executive, another Group executive, and a balanced team of divisional managers.

The Divisional Board should differ from an independent Board in two characteristics only. Firstly, that it does not choose its own Chairman. Secondly, that it does not choose its MD. These appointments must, in all sense, remain in the control of the parent. The divisional Directors are appointed by the Holding Company, which owns 100 per cent of the shares in the divisional company. While they formally 'elect' their Chairman and MD, at their Board, there would be much disorder if they did not simply elect the two choices of the parent – beginning, doubtless, with the removal of those Directors who disagree with the two choices. Here, only, practice can sensibly short-circuit strict legal theory.

If the size and complexity of the parent are such that it cannot pretend to be able to manage by edict through the Group Chief Executive – and it normally cannot – then the Divisional Board must be composed for independent decision making, not just for receiving and disseminating instructions. If the Group Chief Executive, on the other hand, believes that he can in fact manage his empire by a straight-down-the-line mechanism, then he may be in need of a sabbatical. If he cannot extract more by prodding from the side than by sitting at the top, then he is just a boss, not a leader.

Subsidiary Boards

Subsidiary Boards are where it all happens. Where the business is done and the cash is generated. Where the reality of the Group Board's judgement is put to the test. Where the Group grows its future top talent, and the square peg in the round hole is most visibly discomfited. Where returns are most realistically measurable and motivation of men most easily achievable, because performance is most clearly attributable.

But where the executive Directors say the least and are commonly the most frustrated. Where the Board is most frequently a formality, subjected passively to predetermined decisions worked out at a level above, or between the central Directors and the local MD without any involvement of the subsidiary company Directors. Where unproductive resources or businesses are most frequently retained through a whimsical attachment to decisions made in the circumstances of long ago. Where few employees meet a real live Group Director face to face, and where few have any time for, or understanding of, the concept of the non-executive, or of anyone else who is not alongside them with sleeves rolled up.

It used to be believed that the primary motivation of men was money. It may still be with that rare and valuable animal, the 'born salesman', and in some cases with the natural entrepreneur – though he is unlikely to be working for long in the kind of structured environments which we are considering.

But it has been determined that managers are at least equally motivated by 'recognition', and by the opportunity to be recognised. Their greatest needs are often those which are least satisfied: the need for personal growth (not everyone can climb the pyramid); and the need for achievement which the person himself can accept as being real, and as being the fulfilment of what he earnestly believes he is able to contribute.

If Subsidiary Boards, also, were composed and operated as 'real' Boards, there would be an awakening and quickening of contribution from the thousands of down-line Directors who currently sit on their hands. In working with subsidiaries as a Group executive Director, non-executive and consultant, the writer has concluded in almost every case that the subsidiary company Directors had much more to 'give'. Sometimes they volunteer this conclusion themselves, asking if 'something can be done up there' to make their Boards more meaningful. Usually it cannot. Holding Boards understandably, but wrongly, often believe they would lose a large element of control if down-line Boards actually formulated decisions, rather than just accepted instructions.

There is another major advantage to be gained from giving the Subsidiary Board a truly independent role. In the prevailing style of Subsidiary Board, which is a Board only in name, the executive Director does not have to face conflicts within the Boardroom, and so does not develop his ability to handle conflict productively. As he grows, this gap in his experience remains a gap. When he reaches the Holding Board and detects that conflict is likely to arise on a major topic, he will normally run away from it – he is not exercised in doing anything else. Which is one reason why wholly executive Boards, without any outside Directors, can become paralytic.

Conflict will always arise at Holding Board level. It can be funked, or handled productively. The clashing of strong opinions should not be seen as a problem; it can be used as an opportunity.

The world is ruled by force, not by opinion; but opinion uses force.
                                                                  PASCAL

The Board's horror, or the Chairman's horror, of visible conflict stems often from one or two nasty experiences in the Boardroom in the past of a kind which it, or he, has sworn never to go through again. Those experiences proved so painful, not because the subject matter was so sensitive but because the Directors at that time, through their inexperience of Boardroom conflict, handled it so clumsily.

An advantage in having non-executives on at least the more important Subsidiary Boards is that their presence can help the growing executives to exercise their muscles and their tongues productively, not painfully 'clumsily'. They can draw out the Young Turks, without fear or favour, without crossing their lines of command, and without caring a jot about their irreverence as long as what they are saying actually carries the enterprise forward.

The objectives of the next-up level of Board must always be that the subsidiary achieves a set of collectively defined targets by whichever means are most likely to succeed, with the resources which can be made available; then to toughen the targets; thus to obtain more from those resources, and from its senior men. This is not achieved by telling them what to do. They must help work that out themselves. They need to be part of a mix of colleagues which enables, and encourages, them to do so.

Art is I; science is we.

CLAUDE BERNARD

The optimum amount of autonomy for a subsidiary is simply definable: within the Group Board's definition of limits of authority, it should be total. The Group or Divisional Board can always tighten or loosen those limits for each subsidiary separately, in accordance with its results and the demonstrated performance of its management. With some of their own Directors on the Subsidiary Board, they can ensure that things do not gallop away unbridled.

Remote control, which so often means bureaucratic and form-ridden control, can deaden. But remoteness can be turned into a bonus, without diminishing ultimate control, if each adjoining level of Board shares two or three Directors in common, including an independent. Sometimes a Group pushes down too much authority. Management failure down line is not just a failure of down-line managers. Incompetence can be created from above. The limits of senior men can be wrongly measured, even by experts. Hence several should measure them.

The ideal composition for an effective Board in a major subsidiary is just as described for the divisional level. One or two executives, and a non-executive from the level above; subsidiary-level non-executives; a small team of subsidiary company managers; chaired by a non-executive. In smaller subsidiaries there may be only one Director from the level above, but there should still be subsidiary-level non-executives, one as Chairman. There lies a long gradation of skills and detailed responsibilities between the members and the decisions of a Group or Divisional Board and their equivalents on the Board of a subsidiary in a far corner of their empire. Naturally. But people contribute most positively in the same sort of environment, whether writ large or small, and they react and interrelate at all levels in accordance with the same laws of nature. Their Boards, to be effective, need to be composed to the same patterns.

To judge the reality of the benefits to be gained from a more independent composition of Subsidiary Boards, as well as of Boards of smaller free-standing companies, it is relevant to note that:

- in the 7,000 parent companies listed in the volumes of *Who Owns Whom in the UK* there are about 100,000 subsidiaries, or an average of 14 apiece;
- the top 1,500 industrial and commercial Groups account for 85 per cent of the capital employed in the sum of all industrial and commercial companies. These largest Groups contain a higher average number of subsidiaries than the overall figure of 14. The performance of each Group is the sum of the performance of its subsidiaries. Group results improve when subsidiaries' results improve;
- in the 'Size Report' on the 4,000 largest holding or free-standing companies in the UK it is strikingly demonstrated that the smallest of these perform much less well than the largest. The top 50 of the 4,000 average £4,228 profit per employee per annum, and the smallest 50 of the 4,000 average only £573, with a gradual, if not entirely smooth, decrease observed from top to bottom.

All levels and sizes of company are bound by the same laws. The legal niceties do not normally cause any bother until a subsidiary runs into trouble and a parent decides to liquidate, or to dissolve without liquidation; both of which situations are likely to increase in frequency.

Many a Group has created spurious subsidiaries in order that a large number of senior employees can put the title 'Director' on their visiting cards. In at least one major City Group, over 10 per cent of all employees are Directors of subsidiaries whose Boards meet only once a year, and then only to fulfil the formal requirements of the Companies Acts.

The value of this sales aid, or ego booster, must be balanced against the dangers that a client may view the person with such a position as genuinely responsible for more than the Group wants him to be responsible, or that at time of subsequent dissolution that person truly is enmeshed in more than he was intended to be concerned with.

Anyone about to become a Director of a subsidiary company, and most particularly of a nonsense subsidiary of this kind, would be well advised to go through the company's Memorandum and Articles, and Companies Acts of 1948, 1967, 1976 and 1980, and then have a close look at any guarantees or commitments which exist between the company and the Group, or any other part of the Group. He must understand the theoretical and legal situation into which he is about to place himself. Practice may differ from theory today; but what about tomorrow?

The law on the relationship between parent and subsidiaries is certain to change under pressure from the EEC, and properly so. It must be inherently 'wrong' that the House of Lords could rule in 1980 that, in accordance with current law, Lonrho could not force Shell and BP to disclose certain documents held by some of their subsidiaries on the grounds that these documents were not 'in the power' of the parent companies.

Some inroads have been made into this concept of wholly separate entity, even in the UK. For example, the tax laws require disclosure and consideration of subsidiary company results as an integral part of the parent's situation. In contrast, under current UK insolvency laws the parent and its subsidiaries are treated as completely separate legal entities, subject only to any collective guarantees which the bankers may have required when they began to sense that trouble was brewing. Under these laws a Group itself may be eliminated, while some of its subsidiaries may continue their existence, either independently or within another Group. The creditors of the Group may receive nothing at all; the creditors of one subsidiary may receive 90p in the £. Current UK law helps the taxman, but not always the creditors nor the minorities.

The individual Director may consider the legalities of corporate relationships irrelevant to daily operations, or that the threat of insolvency is too remote to cause him concern. But his own relationship with subsidiaries, and the attendant responsibilities, may not be so remote.

Under the concept of the 'shadow Director', now formally recorded in the Companies Act of 1980, an individual Director's responsibilities can run down the line (section 63(1)):

> Subject to subsections (2) and (5) below, a person in accordance with whose directions or instructions the directors of a company are accustomed to act ('a shadow director') shall be treated for the purposes of this Act as a director of the company unless the directors are accustomed so to act by reason only that they do so on advice given by him in a professional capacity. [Subsections (2) and (5) relate to banks and bodies corporate.]

The Director, and particularly the line executive Director, has to view his responsibilities by looking 'downwards', also, below the level of the Board to which he is formally appointed. Parent and subsidiary company Directors, for example, can run the risk of being charged with 'conspiracy to defraud' if the parent controls a subsidiary through its nominated Directors and they carry on a business which is insolvent. This is not some minor technicality which need cause little concern, as many Directors might discover if they tease apart the current situation of all their subsidiaries, including those little nuisance companies which never rate a mention at the Board.

EEC proposals on a new legal parent/subsidiary relationship are likely to conclude that the subsidiary should support its parent, even against its own interests, with the 'contra' that the parent must carry a joint liability for the subsidiary's debts. This would provide an equitable balance between control and responsibility.

Minorities

Minority shareholders in subsidiary companies prove, more often than not, to be an embarrassment which is best bought out sooner rather than later. They arise most commonly when a Group acquires an independent private company, engages a number of the original Directors, and allows them to retain a percentage of the shares.

The rights of such shareholders are theoretically the same as the rights of minorities in a holding company, though in practice a new parent with as little as 51 per cent in a subsidiary will take decisions affecting that subsidiary as though it was alone. Otherwise it would not have made the acquisition in the first place.

Occasionally a parent will introduce a minority shareholder into a subsidiary for marketing or technical reasons. This rarely works well. If the expertise desired is in the hands of specific individuals to whom the minority stake is offered, then it would be better to introduce such expertise in a consultancy mode. If the expertise desired is in the control of a company to which the minority is offered, then it would be better to establish a licensing or know-how agreement, and otherwise keep at arm's length.

Introducing any kind of business associate to the Boardroom, whether technical or marketing associates, or suppliers or distributors, is bad enough; offering them a minority stake is worse. They reduce the Board's independence in business decision making.

If you cannot escape from having minority shareholders in a subsidiary, with or without Board seats, or with or without a role in daily management, then agree in advance with them, and record, precisely what information they will receive; when they will receive it; what roles, if any, they are expected to play. This will ensure they are kept properly in the picture, without being able to harass a Board which, while acknowledging that in law the minorities must be treated without 'unreasonable prejudice', really just wants to forget about them.

Joint ventures

There can be sounder reasons for establishing new joint venture companies, with shareholdings at 2 x 50 per cent or 3 x 33.3 per cent, than for establishing subsidiaries with minority interests. But in the long term the difficulties posed by most joint ventures, particularly when they remain small, are such that once the initial objectives of the grouping have been achieved, then one dominant partner would do well to buy out the others.

The grouping of equal partners is normally based in the first instance on an observed need to marry market and technical expertise, and perhaps financial muscle, which the separate partners do not encompass individually.

After some years of life the joint venture company will have developed all that expertise within its own separately existing organisation, and the need for a single line of control will become apparent. In almost every joint venture, one partner progressively dominates the decisions and actions of the collective unit. The interests of one will progressively differ from the interests and needs of the others. The difficulty is that the Board of any company, including the Board of a joint venture, is required to base its decision on the interests of that specific company alone. In a joint venture these can come to conflict with the interests of one, or all, of the shareholding partners. The expedient of agreeing, by written contract between the partners, that one will manage and control the joint venture is sometimes used. It will be readily seen that this can only be a temporary expedient; the situation of the joint venture and the interests of its shareholders will change through its history.

A quite typical joint venture history is represented by the case of a 50/50 company in North England, which was established by a UK Group with local market knowledge, and a Dutch Group with both technical expertise in a new field of ultra-heavy haulage techniques, plus a pool of expensive capital equipment usable only for such work. In its first two or three years, with a flush market linked to the North Sea activities, when alternative suppliers with the requisite skills and equipment were few, the objectives in marrying the two interests made sense, and made money. As the market declined, and as competition increased, margins available naturally decreased. The joint venture, which by now contained within itself all the necessary market and technical expertise, could not justify the purchase or replacement of the capital equipment needed to service a very seasonal market. Nor could it justify the purchase of equally specialised equipment for extension out of its originally selected sector of that market. But the equipment could be, and often was, hired from the pool held by the Dutch partner. That partner, however, needed discretion over the pricing of hire, which was the main cost item in this particular business. It needed to be able to choose freely whether to marginal cost in quiet periods, or to make up ground during international peaks, when all potential suppliers were charging high. The joint venture was thus not able to make its own decisions about its own major cost item. The costs, and thus the competitiveness, of the joint venture were in practice controlled by one partner. The only workable solution was for the UK shareholder to sell out to the Dutch, and this was done.

Most joint ventures reach similar situations of conflicting interest. Their Boards, with representatives from each of the partners, and from the senior management of the joint venture itself, usually wait too long to decide on the inevitable concentration of shareholding because of the effect this will have on the individual Directors' positions. Top executives in the joint venture may not be happy with being absorbed into one organisation, which can be felt as moving from real independence to simple subsidiary status. And they may not like the idea of working for the 'obvious' buyer, for one of many possible reasons.

Profitability inevitably sinks as the Board delays taking the decision. Again this is a situation where the involved but independent non-executive – if the joint venture Board contained one, and it seldom does – could take a lead. Only the outsider, who is independent of each of the shareholders, can

humanly ensure that the interests of the joint venture itself
come first, as long as it is alive, and can ensure that the
transfer of control is rational and humane when joint control
is put to death.

Associate companies

The Group's minority stake in an associate company is an
investment. The performance of its investments are seldom
reviewed by the Board as frequently as the performance of
subsidiaries. If one does not control the decisions of the
associate, then there is not much to review except the ROC.

There may be value in having a Director or two on the
Board of the associate; a functional specialist such as the
Finance or Business Development Director, and one non-
executive. Not a general manager, as he could be discomforted
when management decisions are not wholly within his
influence.

If the Group has several associates, it could be useful to
'group' them together under the watchful eye of the same two
Directors, who would report regularly to the Board on actual
ROC achieved compared with planned levels, and compared
with that achieved by the Group's own subsidiaries.

It might be found more sensible to sell out, reduce the overdraft, and boost the growth of the subsidiaries. Or alternatively to increase one's stake in the associate to a majority,
and then boost that new subsidiary. Either way, the stake held
is a commitment of Group resources which needs as much
monitoring and measuring as any other use of resources.

The EEC's proposals for a Eurocompany, last amended in
1975 and still awaiting approval from the EEC Council,
contain some complex rules for situations where the minority
stake exceeds 10 per cent. But where the stake is at or below
10 per cent the proposals require the minority holder to sell
out to the majority company, or alternatively to take shares in
the majority company itself. This is fair confirmation of the
thesis that minority stakes, in subordinate companies, are
seldom worth the hassle to either the minority or the majority
holder.

Diversity

It is simpler to compose, and operate within, a Board concerned with tens of millions of turnover per annum in a uniform business, than it is with a grouping of small companies
selling a few hundred thousands per annum, each, in
differing product categories and markets.

Woolworths (UK) has only one Board to cover the total
activity of 60,000 employees, all in High Street or related
retailing. A grouping one hundredth the size may well have
half-a-dozen Boards, and need them all; it can be more
complex to plan and develop, despite the fact that the
resources deployed are tiny by comparison.

The measure of the task facing the Board is a multiple of the
variables of products, markets, competitors, customers,
technologies, techniques. Size naturally introduces its own
variables, such as the numerous alternative businesses into
which the large Group can afford to diversify. But size can
also provide a balancing, comforting element of financial
flexibility. The smaller, diverse enterprise's problems begin
with fitting the best mix of talents into its Boardroom, while
still keeping the total numbers within workable limits. Specific
expertise has to be concentrated in the executives, most of
them below the Board. Where additional technical support is
required, it is best engaged and employed outside of the
Boardroom; the Board itself will not have the time nor the
space to cover all the detailed knowledge to which the diverse
units need daily access.

In this environment the most useful kind of outside non-
executive Director is a generalist; a strategist experienced in
multi-unit operations; someone who can balance the pros and
cons of the diverse units and help decide dispassionately
which should be built up with the limited resources available,
and which should be run down to make more resources available; who is not devoted to, nor technically enthusiastic about
any one of those units.

This conclusion runs counter to prevailing practice in
smaller, diverse UK enterprises. Technically-based companies
tend to believe steadfastly, even stubbornly, that only men
with from-the-cradle experience in the technicalities of their

specific businesses can be of any use in helping to grow them. Engineering company Boards, including those of very large engineering-based groups, contain predominantly engineering-trained Directors, even when the diversity of specialities is such that no one member can have deep knowledge of more than two or three of the fields covered. They seldom contain broad-based businessmen, strategists, planners, or experienced generalists, either as non-executives, or even as executives.

It cannot therefore be surprising that, while the UK has maintained a high level of research and development expenditure, which has in the past produced a correspondingly high level of innovation: the former British lead in this field has slipped; smaller British companies play little part in such innovation, compared with their counterparts in the USA; and much of the innovation resulting in the UK in recent decades has been exploited profitably outside of the UK, not within it by British companies.

There has long been a close correlation between these unequivocal facts and the continuing imbalance on the Boards of UK technology-based companies, which believe primarily in technical contribution, to the exclusion of purposeful planning, strategic subtlety, and commercial canniness. With a few noteworthy exceptions, the apparent growth of corporations in the UK has been the result of programmes of acquisition, not of any organic vigour deriving from a Boardroom coupling of technical know-how and business professionalism.

If the company's Board is not composed so as to enable and stimulate such vigour, it will not keep pace with competitors which do temper technology with business strategy. It is not coincidental that the British share of world trade in engineering products has been falling for decades, and is still falling.

Funnies

What about that subsidiary in Panama, or the British Virgin Islands? Its original purpose may have been valid, legal, and even decent. It is always quite proper to minimise the unproductive cash-negative of taxation however one legally can, and it is equally proper to ensure that the company has a sound mechanism for transferring monies in all directions with that, or other, business objectives in mind.

The legal ground rules can change, either happily, as in the case of the removal of UK exchange control regulations, which eliminated the need for many of the funnies, or unhelpfully, as they are likely to do in connection with the taxation of inter-national and multinational enterprises. The Board has to ensure that yesterday's mechanism is still the most effective, and is still at least legal.

The wise Director will ensure, firstly, that he knows all about the funnies in detail; who is on their Boards, why, and what they are doing. Chances are that the people concerned have forgotten all about those particular directorships. Secondly, that their activities are reviewed regularly at the Board. The mechanism may be intelligent and acceptable. It may have become rusty or inefficient. Or it may have developed, intentionally or otherwise, into a system whereby the Directors, or some of the Directors, or in a private company some of the shareholders, obtain a higher proportion of personal gain than is equally exposed to all the other Directors or shareholders, or which is not exposed to the taxmen in quite its clearest colours.

The wise Director will accept nothing which is not freely exposed, or not freely exposable. He will not let any element of concern lie 'on the shelf' until a more suitable moment. The only suitable moment is when the concern first arises. The claim, later, that he did not know or did not understand is neither acceptable nor credible, even if true. If he finds that the law is being broken, and he is unable to have this remedied immediately, he must resign. His personal dilemma on such resignation is that other parts of the law state that he cannot bottle up within himself the knowledge that the law is being broken. He is bound to expose known illegalities. Mentioning this fact to his co-directors should usually do the trick and remedy the abuse. But if it does not, he has to expose it. If one bunch of malefactors is not seen to hang publicly, then others will proliferate.

One large international accounting firm which handles a great number of insolvencies has found that fraud is unearthed in about 5 per cent of their receiverships, not always involving overseas funnies, nor even on a scale which contributed to the company's collapse. And it is this last factor which suggests that fraud is therefore present in a small percentage of continuing businesses.

The dangers in breaking the law do not need expansion here. It is the borderline mechanisms which can cause greatest harm to corporate health. Borderline operations are always clearly known to a number of the staff below the Board who handle the paperwork. A progressive decline in morale seeps out of their offices, spreading and multiplying. It can be felt in the air.

The Greek god Hermes, and his Roman counterpart Mercury, were the gods of speed and the patrons of travellers (before the Christians replaced them in the latter role by the good St Christopher). They were also the gods of trade, 'both honest and dishonest'. From well before their time it has been commonly assumed by the layman that the one always contains just a little of the other, even though every now and again demonstrably upright businessmen, such as the Quakers who contributed so much to the development of eighteenth and nineteenth-century Britain, were able to belie the general assumption.

The small pressure groups which currently spend their energies on the iniquities of underpaid workers in Sri Lanka or South Africa could one day turn their attention to the exposable iniquities of that very small percentage of locally-based enterprises which overstep the rules.

Don't wait. If your list of subsidiaries and associates includes the Netherlands Antilles and Norfolk Island, start by asking your own questions about these. There is nothing improper about the helpful services provided by these excellent countries. But there may be about the way a company uses them.

Nationalised industries

The publicly-controlled industries are not controlled by the public; their survival has not been dependent on the quality of their response to the customer. It is not clear what controls them.

By the Acts establishing the nationalised industries, the categories of control vested in ministers were in theory quite similar to those vested in the sum of the shareholders in a company limited, with the addition of control over major capital expenditure, and over borrowings. The ministers were not empowered to instruct nor manage.

So much for the theory. In practice, direct government control, either by ministers or civil servants, is much greater; it varies from time to time and from industry to industry. Sir Monty Finniston's Board at British Steel was not allowed to apply price increases which it believed could generate an additional £750 million, without losing any business. Sir Monty had 19 different ministers to contend with in his ten years at British Steel; Sir Richard Marsh had seven different investment programmes to contend with during his five years as chairman of British Rail.

The roles of the minister and his nationalised industry board have been usefully described as 'a mess of fictions'. Within such unplannable terms of reference, the Boards' Directors can scarcely feel responsible for the strikingly poor performance of those Boards; the eunuch in the harem can hardly be derided for not even wanting to disport himself lustily.

Until the policies and objectives of these industries have been defined, their activities sensibly limited, their plans consistently maintained, irrespective of politics, and until the roles of ministers, ministries, Chairmen and Boards are similarly defined and maintained, these industries will continue to drag down average national performance.

In the terms of reference of this volume, these industries demonstrate in an exaggerated form all the weaknesses of bad corporations in general: bad or non-existent planning, dominating control, and emasculated Boards.

5   Tiers: one, two, many

Who shall guard the guards themselves?

JUVENAL, 2ND CENTURY AD

Every Group of companies already contains several tiers of decision making, including Holding Board, Divisional Boards, Subsidiary Boards, and all the management committees which are positioned through their structures to review and decide a defined range of questions at each tier.

The debate on 'tiers' within the EEC's own machinery of committees, and within relevant industrial and commercial organisations in member countries, centres exclusively on the Holding Board level; on whether or not to introduce yet another level by splitting that one into two. The debate always links the question of having two top-level tiers with the question of having employee or union Directors on the proposed 'upper' tier, the Supervisory Board. The two questions are best considered quite separately.

Whether a company's performance can be aided by introducing a supervisory tier, which watches over management, is a perfectly valid question in itself. Whether that supervisory tier or, for that matter, whether any other level of Board, should contain employee or union Directors, is also a perfectly valid question. But to avoid confusing structure with composition, or confusing politics with performance, this volume will leave the question of employee representation to the next chapter, concentrating here on the structure of the Holding Board.

British and US practice has always been based on the single-tier, or unitary, Holding Board. The law in both countries permits the Board to establish and work through committees, assuming that provision to do so is also contained

69

in the company's Articles. But the ultimate responsibility for the decisions and actions of the committees still rests with the Board which established them, so the practice of one level of ultimate responsibility is maintained.

Proposals from Europe for splitting the Holding Board's responsibilities between two legally separated tiers have been based on the following beliefs that:

- uniformity in all things within the EEC is a good thing. A neat and tidy concept which the average Frenchman must care for as little as the average Englishman, and which we can put quietly aside;
- two tiers have worked well in Germany and some other member countries of the EEC, which have all made demonstrably better industrial progress than the British in recent decades, and
- executive Boards need to be watched and controlled from without their own boundaries, being too often characterised by too little will and courage, and too much self-perpetuating self-interest.

How much reality is there in the last two beliefs?

There has been a two-tier system in Germany since it was first introduced by Bismarck over a hundred years ago. It has evolved to a stage where the 'upper' supervisory tier contains no representatives of management, not even the Chief Executive. It consists of down-line employees, union representatives and non-executives such as bankers – all of them, with the best will in the world, quite remote from the work of the senior managers. Its judgement on proposals of almost any kind which come up to it from the management, including investment proposals, can be based on little more than intelligent ignorance. It can only rubber-stamp, or interfere clumsily. Tease out this question with German executives over a lager or two and they will almost invariably admit that this has been precisely the case for years. The system worked well because the Management Board itself worked well enough for the Supervisory Board to have no real additional business purpose. The incentives for management success in post-World War II Germany, (and in post-World War II Japan) have been stronger, more pervasive, and initially more necessary than elsewhere. Couple this with a natural German ability to plan and methodically implement, and one can conclude that German companies succeeded so well in spite of, not because of, the separation of management from its supposed supervision.

There is something inherently bizarre in creating an extra tier of Board in order to examine and keep in line another level of Board. Who in turn will examine and keep in line the newly created supervisory tier? The shareholders? The shareholders in committee? (The Danes have a few such shareholders' committees.) The employees? The trade unions? The government? None of these groups can act any more directly on, or cooperate any more usefully with, the supervisory tier than they can with the unitary Board.

The implication is that the supervisory tier will not need such external supervision because it will contain two distinct types of person, representing two distinct types of interest, and that each 'side' will not let the other 'side' get away with anything improper. Which means consciously creating adversary roles within a body which, by definition, is intended to have a unified purpose.

Comparing again with German experience, we find that the 'unnatural' dividing of responsibility between two tiers had no ill effects until 1976, when their Codetermination Act was introduced. In this the 'two sides' concept was enshrined in the complicated arithmetic which has been summarised in Appendix II. The motivation behind the arithmetic was clearly political, and it is no coincidence that since 1976 Germany has been experiencing a level and kind of industrial unrest in its major corporations which they had not had to handle before.

It must be self-evident that Boards of any kind fail, however many Directors they actually contain, when they do not contain enough Directors who are able enough, experienced enough, committed enough or courageous enough to press the right kinds of business decision through any barriers, including through a dominant single Director or a placid but permanent majority, or a stubborn self-interested minority.

Dividing the topmost decision-making body must therefore have the very opposite effect to what is needed. It reduces the

competences present within each half. It defines precisely
what is to be done and decided in each, which is another way
of saying that it defines what is not to be done and decided in
each, thus impeding the Director who is willing to give more.
It builds walls between three different kinds of Director split
between two different kinds of Board.

In a UK context it could only be hopelessly destructive. It
would draw attention away from the only structural question
which does have importance: how to compose a grouping of
Directors which, by collective competence and productive
style, can generate improved business performance. The
interests of shareholders and employees alike can only be
protected by improving company performance.

The onus for composing an effective Board does not lie
solely with the Chairman. It lies with each Director, executive
or non-executive. Each is able to detect when his Board is
poorly balanced, or is running out of steam, or is dominated
by self interest. There are always a handful or two of Directors
for every one Chairman, so the main impetus for change
should come from around the table more frequently than from
the chair. It does not. And because it does not the main
impetus for changing British Boards is currently coming from
a variety of sources which themselves have no experience of
operating within such Boardrooms.

The Chairman sits on top of the Board. With unusual
exceptions apart, the man sitting on the top of any structure
is, in the nature of all humanity, the last to decide that true
change is needed. He has to be triggered.

The individual Board still has time to take its own
initiatives to decide and balance its own composition, to
introduce courageous objectivity within its existing single tier,
and to eliminate any chance for the complaint that it is self
perpetuating, self interested, or lacking in will or courage.

The guards may still, just, guard themselves.

6 *Types of Director*

Mix

The average US Board is two-thirds non-executive. The large UK company Board is one-third non-executive. Smaller UK company Boards contain fewer non-executives, and subsidiary company Boards normally contain none.

Within European countries using the two-tier system, some Supervisory Boards, in contrast, contain no executives, not even the Chief Executive. Some contain just the Chief Executive; some also contain the Financial Officer.

Japanese Boards also defy logic (see Appendix I). Before World War II they contained numerous non-executives; today they normally contain only a rigidly structured Board hierarchy of executives. It might be tempting to argue that the success of Japanese industry results, therefore, from its control by self-perpetuating, self-protecting executive Boards which operate without any effective form of internal, or external, monitoring. Such argument would miss completely the real lessons of Japanese success:

– their debt/equity ratios, commonly between 3 and 8, which can fuel a much faster growth rate than is achievable by a UK company working on 0.3 to 1;

73

- their consistently lower bank rate;
- their cooperation between industry, government and lenders, which determines which sectors will be enabled to grow, and which will be allowed to wither through the progressive withdrawal of funding;
- their goal-oriented participation through all levels of their companies;
- their methodical planning and intensive marketing.

Many of these characteristics are already helping Japanese-owned subsidiaries in the UK, Europe and the USA to develop more strongly than most of the native industry.

Boards are a response to their own environment, to the history which has described them, the forces which impel or impede them, and the cultures which encompass them. This is as true for the post-World War II Japanese Board as it is for the galloping-egalitarian Swedish Board. It is as true for the conservative, cautious, complacent and commonly just-too-slow-off-the-mark British Board as it is for the over-reactive, multi-clubbable American environment, where Boards are currently stuffing themselves with almost any minority or specialised interest which troubles to wave a banner outside the Boardroom window for long enough.

One of the first elements of good planning is to have a cold-blooded look at one's strengths and weaknesses, and to work out what one can do about them.

Let us agree that the British are indeed conservative, cautious, complacent and commonly just-too-slow-off-the-mark. If that sounds extreme, let us at least agree that the whole of the rest of the world believes this, and says so to every visiting British businessman, so there's probably something in it. We need to relate that to the roles of Board Directors, and thus to how they can best be composed as a group to overcome these assumed characteristics.

The Board has to:

- analyse, evaluate, decide, plan, instruct, monitor, adapt, monitor . . . and so on round the cycle;
- hire and fire the top executives who implement Board decisions, and who in many cases contribute to their making;

- measure resources, agree their deployment, and define the returns which they must generate;
- structure, organise, communicate, improve;
- look reality in the eye, however uncomfortable this may occasionally be.

It needs people who can contribute consistently to all or most of these processes. Who can see the implications of Board decisions in their effect on the business as a whole; on men, money, markets, methods, all in one.

It needs the Chief Executive, head of the chain of managerial control which runs unbroken from the Boardroom through to the shopfloor itself. It needs the best-experienced Finance Director it can obtain for the money it can pay. It needs a Business Development Director, by whatever title, who can interpret how the market might react to each decision on the agenda, and how the machinery of the company can handle each decision. It may or may not need other functional heads, dependent only on the nature of its business and how often they would actually contribute to decisions – not dependent on how well they have in the past carried out such decisions. Board membership is not a reward for good executive performance.

Beside this core of key executive Directors, the Board needs a number of part-time Directors who do not work in the company, who do not covet anyone else's job, who are not going to play internal politics, who do not owe their careers to being on good terms with the Chief Executive. People who can sit alongside the employed executives, able to judge without fear or favour.

> *A good non-executive director needs to have intellect, integrity and courage. Of these qualities courage is the most important, for without it the other two characteristics are useless.*
>
> ANGUS MURRAY MC

If the part-time Director is to be able to meet the criterion of 'contribution' he or she almost certainly needs to have had Boardroom experience elsewhere. The non-executive role is very different from that of a good executive, different even from that of a good executive Director. The non-executive has to know how to say what the executive Director does not dare say, and that facility can only be learnt the hard way.

The Board needs the key executives, whose whole careers depend on staying with the company long enough to make it a world beater, alongside the part-timers, who can join or leave in accordance only with the Board's own requirements at any stage in the company's growth. It needs a mix of wise old men (not too old); aggressive young men; the cynical; the thoughtful; the men who feel it in their fingers. It needs those with the stomach to say what they believe is right, and to keep saying it until it is adopted or demonstrated to be wrong, or until the nuances of difference have become unimportant. And only such men.

The optimum proportion of professional or personal backgrounds and styles will change as the company changes, as its problems and opportunities vary. It should never be fixed for long. It should never be fixed by legislation. Describing Boards is not a question of fixing numbers, or fractional relationships between numbers, in the manner recorded in the German Codetermination Act of 1976 (see Appendix II), or in the best-forgotten Bullock Committee Report.

Much damage has been done to the evolution of responsible Boards by the attempt to apply such precision to a subject which can never be precise. Even setting guidelines on absolute size can be subject to sensible variations, though anything below five is going to be too small to contain sufficient variety of contribution, and anything above a dozen is going to contain too many non-combatants. Jung believed that group experiences take place on a lower level of consciousness than individual experiences (and that the ethical attitudes of groups are always 'doubtful'). The level of consciousness in a very large Board can approach unconsciousness; there is no Director in any large Board who has not seen a few of his colleagues dozing-off by item 3.

The guidelines on the balance between executives and non-executives are simpler; what does the Board lack? Every Board without non-executives, for a start, lacks objectivity. Non-executives must number at least two, even on the smallest Boards. At times even the non-executive, if alone, can stray from objectivity, and 'desperate courage makes one a majority'. can become quite exhausting. So one-third of the

Board is a workable minimum. If two-thirds of the Board is non-executive there may not be room for the good executives, so this proportion represents a workable maximum for the largest Boards. Between one-third and two-thirds thus constitutes a working range, with fewer non-executives on the smaller company Boards, and more on the larger company Holding Boards.

It is not so much the numbers as the style. A dozen uninterested or complacent non-executives are not worth one with interest and courage. What matters when a Board determines a strategy, describes an organisation, makes an investment, or selects a top executive, is that it has in one forum, around one table, sufficient width and depth of understanding, and caring, to be able to grapple competently with all the aspects of the decision concerned. It needs that the majority of those assembled can state opinions, without personal or specialist interest, which are directed wholly to the objective of corporate advantage. If this means, in any specific company, that the Board must have a non-executive majority because the executives are professionally limited or personally timid, so be it. But if the Chairman is democratic, the Chief Executive a true leader of men, and the executives all experienced and free-spoken, then a non-executive minority will suffice. This happy combination is seldom found.

The Board has to breed a thoroughbred strategy, and it has to feed it and train it and whip it, and win races with it. The breeders and farriers and trainers and riders will be very different kinds of people, bound by the common objective of winning races. And bound by the understanding that they need each other, irrespective even of whether they like each other.

The Chairman

I am not afraid of a knave.
I am not afraid of a rascal.
I am afraid of a strong man who is wrong, and whose wrong thinking can be impressed upon other persons by his force of character and force of speech.

WOODROW WILSON

Democracy in its most literal sense has been common in darkest Africa since long before the Ancient Greeks invented the word. Down to the very smallest hamlet, decisions on daily matters are taken at meetings which all concerned are entitled to attend. Anyone with anything useful to say most certainly says it, and almost everyone else puts in a few words too. Meetings become very long, and would ramble about for ever without a firm hand to control them. So they have someone in charge. Everyone squats on the ground, except the man in charge. He has to be higher up, central and visible. He sits on a chair. It is often just a little three-legged stool. In parts of West Africa the Stool is a lot grander, and has become an object of veneration in itself. But the meaning is the same; the person in that chair is in charge of that meeting.

He is often the wisest, or the wiliest. Sometimes he is just the toughest. He knows his village and his tribe, and he normally has a fairly shrewd idea what is best for them. When he does not, they may starve. His role is to steer discussion, cut short the man who talks too much, and ensure that those he knows have something to say actually get a chance to say it. He summarises the discussion and delegates the actions – but he does not undertake the actions.

He has two other primary functions, one ceremonial and one strategic. In the former he gets carried about looking splendid to the public at large, and providing a focus for local unity. In the latter he leads the closed councils of the elders when matters of survival, such as war or migration, have to be decided on behalf of the clan or tribe as a whole. On these matters the elders make collective decisions. Again he summarises these decisions and delegates the actions, but woe or remote accident betide him who rides roughshod over the elders.

The role of the Chairman in British companies has developed beyond such limitations, and has certainly extended beyond the original intention of the Acts and Statutes which establish such organisations.

The Chairman is the Chairman of the Board. He is not Chairman of the company. There is no such position as Chairman of the company.

By the Companies Acts the Chairman is elected by the Directors from among their number. By the Articles (55, Table

A, 1948 Act) he chairs the general meetings of members, or shareholders, and if he fails to arrive within fifteen minutes of the appointed time the Directors may simply elect another Chairman from among their number present. By another Article (101, Table A) the Directors elect a Chairman for their own Board meetings, and if he fails to arrive within five minutes of the appointed time they may also elect another Chairman. He has in theory no more intended permanence than that.

The Board is allowed to determine, by specific decision, that the Chairman hold that office for a defined maximum period, assuming that he normally manages to be punctual. But the Board seldom does this. The convention has developed that the Chairman is there for as long as he chooses. The convention has also developed that he can perform almost whatever roles he chooses. His roles in fact are:

- to preserve order, and conduct the meetings of the members or Directors in a proper manner;
- to allow members in General Meeting, or Directors in a Board meeting, to have reasonable opportunity to speak, though he himself decides when to curtail further discussion on any point;
- to ensure that decisions are fairly made, if necessary by counting hands or by poll;
- to decide on technicalities, such as the validity of proxies;
- to place a casting vote in the event of a tie;
- to adjourn the meeting if so requested, or agreed by a majority, or if the meeting becomes disorderly. But if he does this improperly, the members may elect another Chairman to continue the business.

Practice has vested in chairmanship duties and powers far removed from this definition of the leadership of meetings.

It is natural, and beneficial to the maintenance of smoothly-working routines in the Boardroom, that the leader of the meetings should retain the chairmanship for as long as he performs the role better than others could do. It is also natural that the public company Chairman, who is visible in the chair at meetings of the members, should become identified as the company's external spokesman, heading discussions with shareholders, the media, analysts and brokers. If he is as good at external PR as he is at conducting meetings, then he is clearly the best man for that role, too. But if he is not good at PR, the Board should put the control of its external relations into another Director's hands. It is allowed to do so.

But there the 'natural' extension of the Chairman's role ceases. Any further extension must depend exclusively on whether or not the Chairman could handle any other roles better than any other Director.

The almost universal convention has developed that all the bucks stop at the Chairman's desk. They do not in law. There is little sense that they should do so in practice. They stop at the Board. The Board may delegate most of the routine bucks to a Chief Executive, and remove him if he mishandles them. The Chairman's role within the Board is to ensure that the responsibilities for all the bucks are clearly defined, and equally clearly monitored. When the Chairman is also the Chief Executive he may feel with a little more reason that he does have to handle all the bucks. One of the dangers in combining these two quite different positions is that the other directors may feel, also with reason, that they carry very little responsibility for anything. There are numerous other dangers. The role of wisely steering a diverse Boardroom towards productive decisions is fundamentally different in character and content from the role of productively implementing those decisions.

A BIM Study in 1972 found that 40 per cent of UK Chairmen are also the company's sole Chief Executive; a further 12 per cent are joint Chief Executive. Fully two-thirds regarded themselves as full-time executives, which de facto would leave the employees, if not the Directors, without any doubt as to who was running the show.

A Korn/Ferry study in 1980, based on companies in the *Times 1000*, found that 45–50 per cent of the sample covered had a combined Chairman/Chief Executive and that, contrary to what is normally believed, the combination becomes more common with increasing size of company, not vice versa. The percentage of Chairmen who had executive duties ranged from 60 per cent in the smaller end of the sample to nearly 90 per cent in the very largest companies. The practice of combining these two roles has thus not reduced during the years between the two studies, despite the welter of argument against it from industry bodies and management experts. And it is even more common in the USA (see Appendix I).

The Chairman leads the Board. The Chief Executive leads the management. The Board holds the Chief Executive responsible for management's performance. It would be naïve to expect that a Chairman who is also the Chief Executive will force his Board to review the performance of management ruthlessly and fire him if that performance is not good. The man is also human. When both roles are vested in one person, no pensionable career executive Director is going to challenge the quality of his bosses' work in open forum. A team of non-executives might. But it is a hundred times harder to challenge the performance of a combined Chairman/Chief Executive than it is to request a review of the performance of two separate people. It is that much harder to demonstrate to the satisfaction of all, particularly to the combined Chairman/Chief Executive, which part of the combined roles is being performed badly. Every reader who has tried it will know that it cannot be done. The situation should not need to arise. The Directors should not let it. The Directors, and they alone, elect the Chairman. And they alone elect the Chief Executive. They are responsible. The Directors should be aware that any strong man will naturally seek to enhance the extent and categories of his power; that is a characteristic of powerful men. The role of the Board is to define and delimit power, and to channel it productively.

Prior to World War II, ICI was dominated by one man. The experience was so traumatic to the Board that it later resolved to ensure that this could never happen again, and the Board recorded a decision that would prevent any future Chairman from also being the Chief Executive.

Some of the larger US and Japanese corporations avoid the problem by substituting for the Chief Executive position a three-man president's office which operates as a single entity. While the original motivation in forming the grouping may have been that three heads acting in unison can manage complex situations more effectively than one alone, it has not escaped them that this also prevents autocracy, the accrued power and roles of this office not being readily re-absorbable, later, by a single dominant Chairman.

In cold logic, the only environment where the combination of the roles of Chairman and Chief Executive can make productive sense is the small, privately-owned company with up to about 100 employees, where the Chairman probably also types the envelopes during a crisis. Certainly once over about 100 employees, the boundary depending entirely on the nature and complexity of the businesses concerned, a separate Chairman will invariably improve the objectivity of the Board, and improve its control of management performance.

The Board may delegate specific duties to any of the Directors, including the Chairman. But it has to formally define and record these, so that there is no misunderstanding. If it does not, who can chastise the Chairman for doing everything, even for doing most of it badly?

His functions besides leading the Board and the general meetings, could possibly be agreed to include heading and organising the following:

- external relations with shareholders and media;
- external relations with the lenders. Certainly. The banks usually have a bigger stake than any single shareholder. But the Chairman would be wise always to cooperate here with the Finance Director who will not wish to be excluded — add the Chief Executive and one of the non-executives if things are tough and the bank has to be convinced that the Board is sound;
- external relations with analysts and brokers. Probably. But the Finance Director might be better at this;
- external relations with governments and civil servants. Possibly. But if any one Director has close working relations with any one ministry, delegate that one to him, not to the Chairman;
- external relations with industry bodies and trade associations. Just possibly. When these organisations are concerned with very broad economic policies, then the Chairman can be a sensible choice, putting over the attitudes of the company, gleaning the attitudes of others, and reporting back to the Board. But where these

organisations are concerned with methods and mechanical questions then the Chief Executive, or maybe the Technical Director, Personnel Director or Production Director could be a better choice. Even when those functions are not represented on the Board, managers can always be co-opted individually to report to the Board;

— external relations with customers and suppliers. Never, except coincidentally, or in a PR combination with another Director more closely concerned;

— internal relations, such as that strange favourite of Chairmen, the house magazine. Never, ever. He is not Chairman of the company;

— other internal functions, such as planning. Seldom. The convention has also developed that the Chairman is the head of planning, and of the definition of strategy. Not so. These are responsibilities of the Board as a whole. Their complexity is one of the main reasons for needing a diverse Board. The Chairman may be a primary contributor, even the cleverest contributor, but he should not be in charge of defining strategy any more than he is in charge of defining tactics. Leave the coordination of these functions to the Business Development Director. If the Chairman is given control of any function which is largely performed outside the Boardroom, albeit finally decided within the Boardroom, he will inevitably encroach on executive territories and create confusion, tension and frustration among the executives. Employees lower down the chain will not sense any confusion; they will simply assume that he really is in charge of the lot. Which he is not;

— balancing the Board. Certainly, but not alone. Yet another convention has developed that the initiative for deciding when the Board needs a face-lift lies exclusively with the Chairman. This leaves him, in most cases, to locate additional or replacement non-executives, and he can hardly be blamed for bringing in his own chums if no-one else is making any suggestions. The captain of the team may be one of the selectors, but he is not the only selector. This may seem the rankest heresy to many a

Chairman, but just pause for a moment and consider the characteristics of power. The Chairman was elected to the chair in the first place because, at that time at least, he was acknowledged by his colleagues as being the natural leader of the Board. Power derives from position. It can be well used and increased, or it can be abused. The powerful Chairman will often be satisfied with a pliant or servile Board, which suits his own purposes, but which is quite useless, or is harmful, to the development of the company. He may not even recognise its destructive servility. Cognitive dissonance, or old-fashioned self-deception, is as common in the great as in the humble. Thus if any Director senses that his Board is inadequate, through age, complacency, incompetence, or conformity, it is his responsibility to seek to effect change through the Board, without waiting for an initiative from the Chairman. It may never come.

Few Directors will take on such an uncomfortable task. The best way to ease the task is to establish five Board routines:

1 All executive and non-executive candidates for the Board shall be vetted by a committee of the Board before presentation to the full Board (see Chapter 9).

2 Each Director appointed shall be given written terms of reference describing the depth and width of his anticipated contribution, and his expected time commitment.

3 The question of Board composition and Board performance shall be given a regular spot on the agenda, at least annually.

4 Each Director, at least each non-executive Director, shall be required to produce a concise report on how he sees the Board's problems and needs, timed to fit in with the annual review of the Board. This report to include how he views his own role.

5 The Chairman shall be required to review the Boardroom performance of each of the Directors with each of them, and to expose his conclusions when the item comes up on that agenda.

Some of the Directors will not like this process, but anything distasteful becomes easier to swallow if it is turned into a habit. If they find they are 'busy men without time for reports and such like', then they are too busy to be much use to the Board anyway. They are not there for the ride; they have to make the horse win races.

Mr Chairman, make your Directors work, especially your non-executives. Give them reports to produce, reports to advise on, staff to evaluate, planning sessions to attend, customers to woo, ministers to hassle, diplomats to charm. Run your Directors and your Board, not the company. Make them speak. That is a start.

The Chief Executive

In the nineteenth century the Boards of UK companies were normally composed entirely of part-time, or non-executive, Directors. Detailed management and commercial questions had to be resolved by formal committees of the Board, or by ad hoc decision by individual Directors. This arrangement became both onerous and clumsy, and led to the concept of delegating daily management to one of the Directors, who would become a full-time employee.

The Articles of most companies now enable their Boards to appoint one or more such Managing Directors, and to delegate to him or to them whatever functions the Board chooses to define, for whatever period and remuneration. Being an employee under contract of employment to carry out these functions, the Managing Director is normally released by the Articles from the requirement to retire by rotation and seek re-election to the Board, which all the other Directors have to do on average every three years. In law he can make decisions or enter into contracts on behalf of the company without reference to the Board. He can similarly sign and seal documents together with the company secretary, who is usually his subordinate, without reference to the Board, except in a very few companies which retain the older requirement that two Directors must sign always.

It will therefore be clear that the Board must not appoint a

Managing Director without defining his limits of authority with considerable precision, or without describing in them the size and type of decision or contract which it requires him to bring to the Board for prior agreement. The Articles will normally refer to the title 'Managing Director', while an increasing proportion of companies prefer to use the alternative 'Chief Executive', a shortened version of the American 'Chief Executive Officer'. But the terms are not necessarily interchangeable. If the Board contains one or several MDs, and if the Chairman behaves outside of the Boardroom as if he is the chief of all the executives, it could be that the Board really considers that the Chairman is also the Chief Executive, and the line boss of the MDs. It all depends on whether the MDs' contracts make them responsible to the Board as a whole, or to the Chairman. If the latter, then the Chairman is effectively the Chief Executive. The term Chief Executive is used throughout this volume because it more clearly describes the role intended. All executive Directors are 'managing' to a greater or lesser extent.

Within the Boardroom itself the Chief Executive is neither 'chief' nor 'executive'. He differs from the other Directors by being the primary link through which instructions for action are passed, and through which results of these actions are reported. Which means he is different as a manager, not as a Director. When the Board judges the performance of the Chief Executive, and perhaps decides to remove him when that performance is consistently inadequate, it is judging his work as a manager, not as a Director.

At the Board meetings he may argue whatever case he feels appropriate in seeking to influence the Board to make decisions which match his own judgement. That is the role of each Director. If the decision, nonetheless, goes against his own judgement, he has to carry it out as best he and his troops can. That is the role of each manager. While his vote in the Boardroom is just one, his arguments will always carry just a little more weight than those of other Directors, and he will always receive a more patient hearing. This places a special onus on the Chief Executive to examine his personal desires or preferences quite clinically, to ensure they are always sharply differentiated in his mind from his judgement of what is really in the best interests of the company.

As an everyday example, the Chief Executive with a Brazilian wife would be wise to ask one of his executive colleagues to present the paper about the proposed acquisition in Brazil, even if that colleague is known to be luke-warm to the proposal. Similarly when the Board of a manufacturing company is debating whether or not to diversify into distribution, and the Chief Executive has spent most of his working life in distribution. Everyone has preferences or prejudices which cloud judgement. In a strong Chief Executive such preferences can become dangerous because of his strength. (And it can be good negotiating tactics, and induce a more sympathetic hearing, if he appears ready to step down a notch and debate from the side, not from the 'top'.)

The Chief Executive may not be, and need not be, the cleverest nor the most experienced of all the Directors. He must, however, be the best leader of men, the best user of men, and a quick and sure judge of the judgements of his key subordinates.

The larger the company, the more easily it is seen that the primary role of the Chief Executive is selecting, positioning, judging, enthusing and using the best men available to him. While he needs to be numerate, and will drown in a welter of tabulations if he is not, he does not need to be a financial expert. But he needs to ensure that he employs a Finance Director who is. He must understand the realities of the market-place, but need not himself be an entrepreneurial innovator. He can employ other executives who are, and can give them free rein under a watchful eye.

And so with the other functions, or areas of expertise, which are important within his particular company. Each of the executive Directors should be capable of sensible consideration for the role of Chief Executive; their specific backgrounds matter little. What matters is that the Chief Executive can extract from men that little bit more than they believe to be their maximum. His ability to control and influence his subordinates is closely related to his visible ability to be influenced by them in turn. He differs markedly from the Chairman, who deals primarily with men of like standing, in that his daily contacts can be with sweepers, machine operators, sales managers and Personnel Directors. His facility for manipulating men is seen, becomes common knowledge, and usually determines the quality of his reputation within the company. Happy is the Chief Executive who has discovered that he gains, rather than loses, stature each time he tells a subordinate in the presence of others that the subordinate's idea is better than his own; successful is the Chief Executive who leads his subordinates round to believing that they thought of it in the first place, because then they will do it better for him.

The good user of men places himself below others.

LAOTSE

The Chief Executive who is slow to 'give away' some of his apparent authority is usually poor at appointing men who are good enough to assume some of that authority. He ends up by insisting he has to do everything himself, in an ever-tightening circle in which he is both the centre and the circumference. Indeed like that mythical bird.

The Chief Executive who begins without the slightest intention of spreading controlled authority will drive away good people, and thus weaken the machine on which the quality of his own performance depends.

The Chief Executive's best friend outside of the Boardroom can be the non-executive who can detect the effect the Chief Executive is having on his team, and can provide a diplomatic suggestion or two.

You can distinguish the Chief Executive who will succeed from the one who may drive you into trouble by determining whether he would rather have a heart-to-heart chat with a good independent non-executive, or go to the dentist.

Other executives

English law recognises the roles of the chairman of the Board and of the managing director, but describes no other differences between Directors. Within the Boardroom all Directors are intended to operate as equals, without 'executive', 'non-executive', or any other categories of differentiation.

The Board is free to choose whether and which employees,

additional to the Chief Executive, would be useful within the Boardroom, and can appoint them as Directors, subject only to ratification in general meeting, which is normally readily given. Once within the Boardroom, such employees are released from the daily hierarchy, and no stigma must attach to the executive Director who disagrees openly with his line boss at the Board table, assuming naturally that what he says is sensibly and soberly expressed.

There are few limitations regarding who may become a Director. The law itself disqualifies the following:

- undischarged bankrupts, unless authorised specifically by the court (they cannot be managers either);
- persons specifically prohibited by the court for a defined period, because of conviction for a variety of company or criminal offences;
- the auditor of the Group or of any of its subsidiaries – he also may not be an employee;
- a clergyman;
- a person over seventy years old (unless in an independent private company, or public company, the Articles of which expressly provide that he can; or unless the general meeting of members agrees that he can);
- the company secretary from being the sole Director of a private company.

The Articles of Association may disqualify whatever categories the shareholders wish to exclude, and may also restrict membership of the Board as narrowly as shareholders choose. Once the Articles are adopted it needs a 75 per cent majority to alter them, so a company would be wise to leave its catchment as wide as possible and disqualify in the Articles only:

- persons below 18 years and above 65. Extend to 70 only for holding companies which operate through comprehensive Divisional Boards. Elsewhere use older men, if judged helpful, as external advisers;
- persons of unsound mind.

The commonly required share qualification, which can usually be satisfied by the transfer of a single share, may seem

more trouble than it is worth. But it can prove helpful to the
Director himself to have formal member status, for example if
he later concludes that he should stimulate the shareholders to
take a court action against the Board. The law regarding who
may take action against the Board, for what, is involved and
evolving. On balance, the share qualification is worth retaining, at least until that law has been clarified.

Given that the company should keep the predetermined
qualifications and disqualifications for Board membership as
few as possible, the Board should only consider appointing
those executives whose contribution can be expected to cover a
wide range of Boardroom topics, not just subjects within an
executive's own specialist field. If the Board concludes that a
key executive is unlikely to be able to contribute freely on most
agenda items, but that his specialist knowledge is needed from
time to time in the Boardroom, he can be co-opted ad hoc.

There are several categories of executives whose contribution is most likely to be needed frequently, and thus who are
the more obvious contenders for a directorship.

The Company Secretary

His situation can be a little awkward when he is not a
Director. The law recognises him as an officer of the company;
he attends all the Board meetings, and drafts the minutes for
the Chairman. Some argue that his daily functions are so
detailed and specific that in practical terms they exclude him
from an active role in the broader strategic deliberations
which characterise the agenda. Others, that as he sits there all
the time, and is privy, if not party, to every nuance, he might
as well be a Director. He is very much the keeper of the
Board's conscience, as well as being the keeper of its records,
and he is the prime internal source of legal information affecting Board decisions. Sometimes the question is solved by combining the roles of Finance Director and Company Secretary,
though the functions of the two are quite different in
character. Decision on this question, as indeed on the question
of any appointment to the Board, should be made on the
principle that a man's personal qualities and personality are
much more important than his specific background. If still in

doubt, he is better in than out. One of the most effective Directors whom the writer has met, with the knack of always putting his finger on the critical factor in any complex case, happened to be a Company Secretary. This knack would have been of equal value to the Board if the man's daily role had been quite different.

The Finance Director

The least problematical appointment to a Board is that of the Finance Director and yet 8 per cent of the Boards of the largest UK companies do not have one (see Appendix I). The Board needs within it a well trained and widely experienced accountant who is up to date in all the intricate details which fall within the finance function. Most of the other directors are ignorant of these intricacies, and often a little frightened of them. While it can be possible to obtain this type of expertise in the form of a specialist non-executive, it can only be of practical value to the Board if it is being applied daily in all the corners of the company, thus ensuring that contribution in the Boardroom combines theory with detailed knowledge of the actual situation of the businesses encompassed. Chapter 8 shows that the absence, or inadequacy, of Board-level representation of the finance function is one of the characteristics of companies which collapse.

The Business Development Director

He is called by a variety of titles, including Marketing, Planning or Sales Director, depending mainly on which part of the total function seems most important in the company concerned. Terminology has become confused. The word 'marketing' today has as many different definitions as the word 'socialism'. Sometimes the Head of Sales reports to the Head of Marketing. Sometimes vice-versa. Sometimes a Board separates the roles, and contains several bodies individually representing sales, marketing and planning. The roles are, however, completely interrelated. It is most effective to arrange that the heads of each role report to a single Business Development Director, who controls the total function. The roles have the common factor that they are all most directly concerned with the realities of the market-place, even planning. A plan has no reality unless it is directed at using the characteristics of the markets to achieve defined objectives; unless it is composed in relation to the competition in those markets. 'Sales' is in the middle of the markets; marketing and planning are one step removed, mapping out how and where sales should be hunting, and weighing alternative returns.

All the strategic, investment and organisational thinking carried out by a Board must, if it is to have any value to the company, be directed to the task of making a defined number of sales, at defined prices, to a defined clientele, against a defined competition, at defined costs and to a defined timescale. The Board which is without an executive Director experienced in these roles will therefore be depriving itself of the expertise on which the company's survival entirely depends. Only the Holding Boards of the largest Groups, which operate in practice through comprehensive Divisional Boards, might sensibly feel that they do not need to include this function within their Boardrooms. Of the Boards of the very largest UK companies 56 per cent still wisely include a Marketing or Sales Director, which compares with 80 per cent only of the Boards of medium to large companies.

The Personnel Director

Of the smaller companies in the *Times 1000* 12 per cent have a Personnel Director on the Board, rising steadily to 58 per cent of the largest companies. The increasing appointment of Personnel Directors to British Boards through the 1970s was a reflection of the volume and complexity of new employee-related legislation which was introduced in that decade, as well as a reflection of the ever present threat of industrial unrest. Quite apart from this unhappy need, the Personnel Director can also provide a useful counter-balance in Boards where the Chief Executive is by nature insensitive to people.

The Production Director, and related technical functions

Appendix I records data on the frequency of appointment of other executives to UK Boards. The data can be a little mis-

leading in the case of larger companies, where specialist functions are more commonly represented on the Divisional
Boards, which control the normal business of the group.

The criteria for appointing these, or any other Director to
any level of Board are whether they will add to the skill or
style of the Boardroom, and whether they will, professionally
and personally, improve the company's performance by
helping to improve the Board's decision making.

The criteria of the law regarding the performance of all
Directors are in addition that:

- they must act in 'good faith' for the benefit of the
  company;
- they must ensure that what they are doing is relevant to
  the company's business; and
- they must act with 'skill and care' in the interests of the
  company.

While court action against Directors is still rare in the UK,
it is very common in the USA, where damages for breach of
duty or other failings can be substantial. Few Americans will
join a US Board without first receiving confirmation that the
company's indemnity insurance for all Directors is large
enough, and is paid up to date. In the UK, few companies or
individual Directors carry such insurance. They will soon
want to. American practice has a habit of drifting over to
Europe. The Board could usefully begin to make enquiries
about such insurance policies.

Standards of 'skill and care' were low in the nineteenth
century, when Directors were non-executive, and were
apparently not expected to know much about business. Case
law in the UK has stiffened this criterion to the point at which
the standard of skill expected from an individual Director is
defined as the level of skill which someone with his particular
knowledge and experience might be expected to exercise.

It can be concluded that, in the event of court action against
Directors, the standards of skill expected from a Finance
Director FCA, or a Production Director FIProdE, in matters
related to their specialist fields, could be set high. This is
something that Boards should keep in mind when measuring
executives for directorships.

Associates and alternates

The complexity and extent of the Director's legal liabilities, together with the certainty that these will become more painfully apparent with time, bring into question the wisdom of the concepts of Associate and Alternative Directors. Both categories can be created by the Articles of a company, but they are not included in the standard provisions of Table A of the 1948 Companies Act.

The Associate Director, sometimes called Assistant, Regional, or Special Director, or a similarly qualified title, is not a member of the Board. He has been given the title of 'Director' to enhance his internal or external status. The danger can arise that external third parties believe, and are entitled to believe, that such a person really is a Board Director, and is therefore empowered to undertake commitments which are not in fact within his defined responsibilities. He could also be viewed as a de facto Director in the eyes of the law; someone not appointed to the Board but 'occupying the position of Director', and thus bearing all the responsibilities, and liabilities, of a properly appointed member of the Board. The device of giving a faithful servant who is close to retirement, or who is not quite suited to Board membership, an Associate directorship, could be more safely replaced by some tangible, and less risky, form of thanks.

The Alternate Director is appointed by an existing Director to represent him during periods of absence. For the length of such periods the alternate is a de facto Director, with full directorial responsibilities. The device is most commonly used when one Director's absence from a particular meeting, for whatever reason, may swing a crucial vote, or when that Director is permanently overseas, or travels so often that he cannot attend most Board meetings. If the debate he will miss is so critical, he can always find a suitable 'proxy', or can tell the Chairman in advance how he would place his particular vote. Few Boards will discount his opinion on a technicality if he troubles to make it clear in advance. If he is so frequently overseas, or is permanently based in Australia – and there are examples of the latter case in major corporations – the Board almost certainly does not need him at all. Or else it needs someone like him who can perform the particular role properly and fully.

The responsibilities of directorship are not to be switched on and off like a ceiling fan.

The old retainer

Employees below Board level are normally required by their terms of employment and the inter-linked company pension scheme to cease working at somewhere between 60 and 65 years (in Japan at 55). Pressures to streamline overheads through early retirements are relentlessly pushing down the average. But Board Directors, like judges, can go on for ever, if the Articles are so kindly couched (the same is true in Japan).

The 1948 Companies Act intended that public company Directors should not be older than seventy, but it allowed the Articles or a General Meeting to alter this limit. No limit was placed by the Act on private companies, though they can choose to introduce their own defined limits by specific provision in their Articles.

Data on Board age characteristics are scarce, and the excellent annual studies of Boards carried out by Korn/Ferry in the UK and the USA coyly omit 'age' from their questionnaires. Some indication of the number of older Directors can be guessed from the number of 'retired' executives and 'previous employees' sitting as non-executives. A BIM Study of 1972 found that 41 per cent of UK Boards contained such retired executives. A Booz Allen study for the Institute of Directors in 1979 found that the proportion of UK non-executives who were 'retired' from full-time roles ranged from 21 to 43 per cent, dependent on the size of the company. In the smaller companies almost two-thirds of these were 'retired' from executive roles within the company itself, with this proportion falling to a quarter in larger companies. The Korn/Ferry surveys of 1980 (Appendix I) came to slightly different conclusions for the UK, but found that 56 per cent of US Boards contained former executives.

One might have expected American Boards to contain a smaller proportion of retired men. They are much readier than the British to fire an inadequate executive, and one could have concluded that they would also be more ready to prune away branches which have done their fruiting. The anomaly is easily explained. Executives are appointed to perform. Non-executives, often, are not. They may be appointed by a dominant Chairman/CEO precisely because they will not. Naturally there are some older men who remain more fruitful and energetic than some of their younger colleagues. But it would be over polite to suggest that they are common. If one counts the bowed and nodding heads around the Boardroom table, one finds that most have long gone grey.

If the old retainer still has some wisdom or specific knowledge to contribute after the close of his executive career, better to use him ad hoc, or as a consultant. (a common practice in Japan). In these roles he can be bolder and blunter, without any need to preserve the niceties of the old hierarchy. A retired executive is seldom truly independent as a non-executive. He can seldom freely interface with his successor, or with his former line boss. Do not keep him in a seat which another could fill more actively more often, just because he occasionally has something useful to say, or because you know his pension alone is not enough to maintain his life-style.

> *Dismiss the old horse in good time, lest he fail in the lists and the spectators laugh.*

> HORACE

You know you cannot decently shout at him when he nods off.

The family

The BIM study of 1972 found that 33 per cent of UK Boards contained non-executives with family or historical connections with the company. Their 1970 study on small and medium-sized private companies had not analysed this particular question, though the proportion of family connections on the Boards of smaller private companies is undoubtedly higher.

A heavy proportion of family representation on the Board and in the management is natural with an embryonic or still young organisation, where directorship goes together with shareholding and the first stages of capital risk. But when the company reaches a size of about 100 employees – or higher or lower, depending on the nature and complexity of the business – it begins to need a good measure of professional management expertise, and experienced business judgement, sitting alongside the entrepreneurial flair of its original driving force, which is usually just one person, and rarely more than two in tandem.

Close relatives may or may not have that expertise and judgement. Statistically speaking, they are unlikely to be the best equipped people available to fit into slots on the Board. Continuity and the thickness of blood may add something to commitment, but it is a lot harder to fire cousin Charles if he is incompetent.

The maintenance of control by one family is seen also with some large, publicly quoted enterprises which have the ability to choose their Chairman, Chief Executive or other Directors from the whole international pool of talent in commerce and industry. By the time that a company has 'gone public' and reached such size, the statistical probability that the younger members of the family are the best available people for these positions is clearly very small. True, they just may be, and with such large public corporations there are also large public shareholders who have enough weight to initiate change if performance is poor. At least if they trouble to. Such shareholding is external to the Board, and can pressure it freely.

Not so with the majority of private companies where shareholders are dominant within the Board. Any external pressure for improvement in performance, which so commonly equates with pressure for improvement in the Board's composition, must come from the lenders. Their 'pressure', however, is normally confined to a comment or two to the Chairman, passingly made and seldom pursued. The standpoint of most of those lenders which concentrate on supporting smaller companies has been confirmed to be that: 'we provide advice, and if the shareholders don't take it and go bust, that is their prerogative. It's their money'. But it is not, and it is not, respectively.

The state, with its stake in the pre-tax profit, has a larger interest in the company than anyone, not forgetting PAYE, NHI, VAT, contribution to GNP, import substitution, and the avoidance of having to pay unemployment benefits. The creditors' stake, and the lender's own stake in the company, will also exceed that of any one shareholder, or of all of them together.

It is not the prerogative of shareholder Directors or family Directors to let the company become insolvent through an over-prolonged indifference, or through professional inadequacy of cousin Charles and nephew Norman, or through the now legally outdated belief that if you own the shares in the company you can do with it what you will. You cannot. It would greatly help performance in the small company sector if the lending bankers made a routine of repeating this to the Board of the family-oriented company, which on the one hand enjoys limited liability, and on the other hand employs real people.

The maverick

In Texas in the middle of the nineteenth century a certain Samuel A. Maverick was found to be accidentally in the possession of a number of unbranded cattle. The term 'maverick' came to be used in the cattle districts for any calf or yearling without an owner's brand. And in time it came into general usage as a description for someone who has no master, or who behaves as though he has none.

In the USA the maverick may be viewed with caution, but also with a measure of respect. In a land where rugged individualism has so often created strength and wealth out of nothing at all, the man who vigorously differs is something of a folk hero. Assuming, of course, that he is also a performer, not just an eccentric. The American grows up in an environment where it is normal to form rapidly a large number of loose attachments, to join a large number of social or commercial groupings, and to dissolve such allegiances equally rapidly, without any stigma attaching to his doing so.

The UK environment is quite different. Team spirit is the

corner stone of cooperation, which is largely geared to cooperating with those who play in the same kind of team, or at least to the same rules. The British form fewer attachments, more slowly and more deeply. They join fewer groupings, and consider membership a bond. Within such groupings the maverick has little room for manoeuvre, if indeed he ever gets in.

The American executive who falls out with his company, with either his line boss or his Board as a whole, will readily find alternative employment if he can show that personality or policy were the genuine reasons for his departure, rather than any failure in his own professional performance.

In the UK, such a man is 'dead'. This characteristic flaw in UK corporate judgement has been confirmed by psychologists and recruitment specialists who work on both sides of the Atlantic. Quite apart from the damage which it may have on potentially useful men, it can also harm the company in two ways. Firstly, it can deny to the company or its Board the very style of input which it most needs to avoid seizing up. It institutionalises similarity and conformity, and it minimises innovation and change. Secondly, it means that the thousands of in situ executives who recognise this corporate characteristic will strenuously avoid any behaviour which smacks of the maverick, irrespective of whether or not their own wits tell them that the moment is ripe for a measure of expressed dissent or purposeful abrasion. They will let the fertile moment pass, and the corporation will not benefit, nor learn, nor change. It will freeze into conformity, which outwardly is the twin of complacency. In the absence of an element of irreverence, all groupings, including the Board, will sink into passive submissiveness.

The maverick does not conform. He is idealistic, as well as individualistic. He is confident, which adds to the discomfort he can cause in environments which are inherently fearful, and which will become more fearful as the external environment becomes more demanding. He is loyal to the objectives of the corporation, but is insubordinate, aggressive and impatient when it takes its eyes off those objectives.

He can be a bit of a corporate pain. Pain stimulates.

The court jester

The role of the court jester, or Fool, has been traced in England to well before the conquest of 1066. He was chosen for his quick intelligence and acute perception of human characteristics, and was licensed to speak to or about his superiors with a unique freedom. This freedom was not absolute, and the risk he could still run in playing his role led him often to use riddles rather than cutting comment.

The role was not solely negative, nor simply to make fun of the foibles of established pomposity. He was to act as an uninhibited sounding board for his king, who was otherwise surrounded by subordinates and sycophants. He clothed himself in a coat of 'motley', composed of patches of past garments. His weapon, apart from his wit, was the 'bauble', a stick with an inflated balloon-like bladder at one end. With this he would strike his victim of the moment. But without hurting. Sometimes he overplayed his hand and suffered dismissal or the stocks. Seldom worse, because his activities were accepted by all as being of positive intent.

Charles I was the last British monarch to have a court jester. But instead of a wise Fool, he engaged Muckle John, a simpleton, thus downgrading and effectively eliminating the role in England. We all know what happened to Charles I.

The same downgrading of the role of the Fool had occurred in the period when the power of republican Rome gave way to the weakness and degeneration of imperial Rome. Progressively the canny adviser gave way to the imbecile, and his whole purpose was perverted. In France, also, from the fifteenth to the early seventeenth century, the role of the Fool became wholly negative. Societies of Fools were made up from groups of priests who satirised their leading contemporaries by dressing up in learned gowns at the annual Festival of Fools, and then derobing to expose the motley beneath. There was an annual secular equivalent which centred on having a good laugh at the affairs of the appointed Lord of Misrule.

Rather like the Board having a collective chuckle at the developing idiosyncrasies of the Chairman or Chief Executive, without doing anything positively helpful about them. Any person in a position of eminence will develop idiosyncrasies.

They come with eminence, and are exaggerated by it. Which is why mediaeval kings and Roman emperors did what the Fool indicated to keep them in check.

The Fool was naturally a godsend to the writers of his day. Shakespeare used him three times to memorable effect. Feste in *Twelfth Night* simply highlighted the follies of men. Touchstone in *As You Like It* satirised the behaviour patterns of society. But in *King Lear* the Fool moves steadily downwards through the play from the role of desperately helpful adviser to but a painful chorus of the king's deepening personal tragedy. *King Lear* was written in 1606 when there was a mood of general despondency throughout England. Elizabeth I had died in 1603. Public finance had fallen rapidly into chaos after her death. A flush of indiscriminate knighthoods and related preferences had been carelessly granted by the new king. The Gunpowder Plot of 1605 had failed to blow up all the decision makers. Since 1604 the country had been in the grip of a general depression.

A disquieting but familiar scenario, in which the Fool moves from the simplicity of truth and common sense to ultimate despair. He had tried to help his king by advising what could be done more wisely. His king did not want advice, lost his daughters and his sanity. And his Fool. Perhaps Shakespeare also intended that there should be a moral in all this.

Non-executives

There are experienced men who believe that the non-executive Director (or 'part-time' or 'outside' Director) is quite useless. There are others who believe, equally strongly, that a wider or more active use of non-executives is the single most important change which Boards in commerce or industry can make to improve the overall standards of performance of their companies. Both beliefs can be supported by real-life examples. The non-executive has often been proved to have been unable to prevent corporate collapse. Companies large and small, publicly visible or hidden away, have fumbled along for years, or else died noisily, while carrying Boards resplendent with some of the most prominent names in the corporate world as their non-executives.

The non-executive can also prove harmful. When fundamentally ignorant of the detailed situation of the company on whose Board he sits, he can do little more than judge superficially on any question of critical conflict, and then place his vote on the criterion of where the centre of gravity appears to lie. Or on some more honourable criterion which may be equally wrong.

The reader must be left to think of his own examples, good and bad; but everyone has read about Burmah Oil, Rank, EMI, Rolls-Royce, Alfred Herbert, Leyland in its many incarnations, and a host of banks and financial institutions in the mid-1970s. Their sagas are being repeated in countless other Boardrooms, right now.

It is not that the concept of non-executive directorship is faulty. Nor even that the individual quality of the people who play the role is open to doubt. It usually is not. The inadequate performance of non-executives results from one or more of the following reasons:

- the selection of the people most suitable to specific Boards at specific stages in their development is misjudged, the process of recruitment used being less rigorous than that applied to the engagement of a clerk – selection is suited to the purpose of the dominant Director;
- criteria for contribution are not established in advance of appointment, and contribution itself is not monitored thereafter;
- the number, and particularly the variety, of non-executives on the Board are insufficient; but primarily because
- very, very few non-executives have spared, or even been able to spare, enough time to their non-executive roles to get to know their companies well enough to be able to contribute anything of the remotest value to the companies' prosperity.

The Korn/Ferry studies of 1980 confirmed that the average UK non-executive contribution amounts to about one day per month, with a similar average applying to the American non-executive.

The BIM's 1972 study found that:

> A non-executive Director rarely gave more than two days a month to his company and half the companies with non-executive Directors expected them to give only one day or less. Given that it will probably be at least a year, and probably two, before a non-executive Director has a sufficient grasp of his company's affairs to make a real contribution, and that even then he will only see Board Papers, attend on average monthly meetings and make occasional visits to the company's establishments, his influence must necessarily be limited.

It has been separately confirmed by practising non-executives that, at this rate of contribution, it does indeed take well over a year to be able to add anything useful to a Boardroom's deliberations. When we take into account that the appointment of the non-executive is made against an observed need in the Boardroom, often quite urgent, it is proper to ask:

> From what other adviser, consultant or profession would the Board, or its management, accept, and pay for, such a long period of non-contribution?

Within larger companies the managers are accustomed to sitting alongside non-executive co-directors, and are well aware that most of these are in no position to be able to query or threaten entrenched positions.

Within the predominantly or exclusively executive Boards of small or medium-sized companies, which have the greatest need for active non-executive contribution, there is commonly great resistance to the appointment of non-executives. Not always – the high-flyers with their eye on the top of the ladder will sometimes welcome such colleagues as an aid to their own exposure. But, coupled with an element of concern about the probing of executive performance which the non-executive is supposed to introduce, there is the strikingly widespread belief that, on the hard evidence, the non-executive is not able to 'add anything'.

The only valid reason for introducing non-executives to a

Board is that they can 'add' by doing what the executives cannot, or can add to what the executives alone can only partly achieve. This includes:

- providing objective evaluation of the businesses of the company;
- providing unprejudiced evaluation of the real performance of the Chief Executive and other key managers, both within the Board and downline. This can be the most important role where the Chief Executive dominates his colleagues for either the right or the wrong reasons, and is a role which no executive Director can be expected to carry out with 'true' judgement;
- providing independent opinion on questions of strategy, investment, divestment, structure, internal relationships, limits of authority, budgets ... these opinions being uninhibited by considerations of career, status or personal empire, and thus often likely to differ greatly from prevailing executive opinions;
- providing experience of the external environment – markets, methods, competitive practices, governments – which can provide either new knowledge or a new standpoint from which to view the same knowledge;
- providing, especially to the small or medium-sized company, new expertise in professional or management techniques, in technical or financial disciplines, or in the evaluation of business performance or business alternatives;
- providing a pool from which the Chairman or his successor can be appointed, and providing when necessary a check on the Chairman himself. They recognise when the emperor has no clothes, and can tell him. It helps no one if he catches pneumonia, and the executives will certainly not comment.

They can also be used by the Board in:

- providing additional or better links with external organisations, as well as internally; creating confidence among investors and lenders; carrying out whatever monitoring or support exercises the Board may choose to delegate to them.

Even in the very largest organisations, where the team of top executives may well know as much about the external environment as the company can need to know, and where they can provide all the necessary expertise, professionalism, and clear-headed analyses, there will still be a great deal of executive in-fighting which needs independent refereeing. There will also be a marked shortfall of independent objectivity among the full-timers.

Harry Roff, who founded and led MSL, the world's largest executive recruitment company, has stated that: '. . . less than one in four executive Directors have this capacity for critical objectivity – largely because of the pressure and influences of their executive duties'. The extent of these pressures and influences was measured some years ago in a European study, which demonstrated that the maximum time that an executive is left on his own during a normal business day is 14 minutes. The maximum time without interruption was found to be nine minutes. Which illustrates neatly the natural difficulty faced by an executive in switching from the exercise of his practical daily role to the cerebral objectivity of the Boardroom, and back again.

It also forces the question of how many full-time executives can sensibly be considered as potential non-executives for other company Boards. How many can make the switch? How many (of those whose companies will release them) can release themselves? The full-time executive who is able to spare the time from his daily role; who is allowed to spare that time, without spasmodic hindrance by his employing company; who is already well experienced in working at Board level, and who is freely able, by competence and character, to impart of this experience to another company in another environment, can be a valuable non-executive. But if he 'is not' any one of the above, then he would serve all parties best, including himself, by confining himself to his executive role.

The pool of full-time executives is the most obvious source

of potential non-executives. There are other pools, both existing and developing, which will be considered in the following
sections. The Board which is searching for non-executives
should dip into all the pools. It should balance its mix of non-
executives as carefully as it balances the total number of outsiders against the total of in-house executive Directors.

With Board size ranging from five to twelve, and with the
proportion of outsiders ranging from one-third to two-thirds,
then Boards are looking for between two and eight non-
executives apiece. Consider a hypothetical, middle-of-the-
range Board of a medium-sized company, with a total of eight
Directors, half non-executive, and with the four in-house
Directors including the Chief Executive, the Finance Director,
the Business Development Director and the Engineering
Director. It has a non-executive Chairman, who used to be a
Chief Executive in another company, and who is now Chairman or non-executive in a handful of separate companies. It
has three other non-executives.

There is not much point if all three are full-time executives
elsewhere, with similar backgrounds to the Chairman, and to
the company's own Chief Executive. Five similar backgrounds, plus three executives, does not bring in the variety,
nor create the productive mix, which was considered in
Chapter 1. Having, say, four working Chief Executives on one
Board can be counter-productive. Their daily work is giving
orders and taking specific and individual decisions, neither of
which they can do in the Boardroom. They either bring their
power drive with them, in which case the Boardroom becomes
a shambles, or, more frequently, they sit quieter than all the
others, being 'out of context'.

> *Appointing a Chief Executive from outside as a non-executive can
> bring problems into the Boardroom, particularly if it is a new
> experience for that individual.*
>
> G. H. G. HARRIS,
> CANNY BOWEN & ASSOCIATES

If this were not the prevailing situation, then there would be a
lot less complaint about Board performance in the USA,
where they dip deeper into the pool of full-time executives and

Chief Executives to obtain their non-executives than is common, yet, in the UK.

In the hypothetical Board which has been considered, two of the outsiders might usefully be full-time executives in other companies, from two separate disciplines – for example a Finance Director and a Marketing Director. They should be Directors elsewhere, not just executives. Directorship is far removed from managing. The other two should be quite different. Compounding a fertile mix of non-executives is just as important as balancing the team of in-house managers who are selected for the Board. They can be chosen from the catchments of consultants, academics and professional Directors, which are the widest and deepest of all catchments in the variety of backgrounds, styles and skills which they can provide. But these two, also, must have demonstrated successful Board-level experience.

Directorship is work for teachers, not for trainees.

Not . . .

The dos and don'ts for composing the non-executive team apply as well, and with as many sound exceptions, to all levels of Board, except the Holding Boards of the very largest corporations. These differ by being remote from detailed company management, which they leave to their Divisional Boards. How they compose themselves may reasonably vary from these guidelines. How their Divisional Boards compose themselves may not.

The Board may sensibly consider whom it will as a potential non-executive Director, but:

Not the company's banker or merchant banker, per se. If there is one on the Board who bubbles over the brim with good ideas about the new venture in Venezuela, or even about the management succession in Manchester, and who by nature defers to no one, terrific. But if he is there because the Board needs advice on funding, or seeks goodwill in the City, then the company would benefit by engaging a more skilful finance Director instead. Any ad hoc requirement for very special forms of financial expertise can be hired by the day. The proportion of US Boards with such non-executives is steadily decreasing.

Not lawyers who provide services to the company, nor brokers. The proportion of US Boards with this category of non-executive is also decreasing. In the UK between 5 and 22 per cent of non-executives are practising lawyers, the proportion varying by company size (Booz Allen 1979). Are they also business strategists, or management experts?

Not representatives of connected businesses, such as suppliers, customers, distributors. The Board cannot sensibly open to them its management accounts, competitive trading problems and price build ups, let alone its deeper long-term thinking.

Not retired executives from the company, nor from other companies, unless they retired young in order to play this kind of role.

Not retired civil servants or diplomats, unless they have spent some part of their careers at senior levels in commerce and industry and really understand what it is all about. Their experience of chairing or sitting on committees bears no relationship to chairing or sitting on a company Board. They are not going to start learning new tricks at 65. If they truly have some contacts in the right places which the Board has determined must be actively cultivated, then invite them to dinner with the 'target' and one other Director, and then use that existing Director to pursue the contact. The once 'top' man may be useful for those very qualities which got him to the top, almost irrespective of what he was top of. For these he may be appointed. But the Board which appoints him for the assumed asset of the contacts which he made at the top very seldom uses, or needs, those specific contacts. Nearly a quarter of US Boards appoint retired government officials, and the practice has increased in recent years. It makes sense on occasion in the very largest Holding Boards, where the control of the company's businesses lies in the Divisional Boards, and the Holding Board functions primarily as a telescope which concentrates on looking further into the future than an operating Board can pause to do.

Not retired generals and admirals. If they are still close to the men who purchase the company's missiles and electronic systems, it can engage them ad hoc, also. On commission perhaps. Either they are going commercial wholeheartedly, or they are not, but do not put them on a Board where only one item in ten could have their remotest interest.

Not politicians, unless they too have business experience and are there as businessmen. If you believe you need a politician on the Board in order to get a good hearing in a relevant government department then you really have problems. Again the Holding Boards of the very largest corporations might find their specialist background useful in describing possible future scenarios. Just keep them away from daily realities.

Not people with a 'name', just for the name. If they are there just to decorate the letterhead or dignify the lunch table, forget it. No one is taken in by this any more.

Not a woman just because she is female. In US Boards 36 per cent now contain a 'female' – cf 11 per cent in 1973.

Not a coloured man just because he is coloured. Ethnic minorities today sit on 18 per cent of US Boards.

Not a local councillor just because he is local.

Nor any other of the curious appointments which many American companies are making to their Boards in the belief that this enables them to take into account the special interests which these appointments represent. One of the large American banks has had a succession of 'student' Directors. They must have some hilarious discussions. The Board is charged with preserving the interests of the company as an entity, not the interests of minorities within the community, nor even the community at large. There are plenty of other laws which look after such interests.

Not anyone who cannot devote to the company an absolute minimum average of two days per month, or who cannot increase this significantly in some months when there is a crisis.

Not anyone who holds more than five or six other

directorships, though loosening the limitation a little for the senior executive of another Group who sits on the Boards of a number of its subsidiaries as a normal part of his executive job. The arithmetic is simple enough. Allowing for holidays, weekends, administration, personal administration and the odd bout of flu, most people can only work productively for about 200 days in a year, executives included. If a Director is devoting a minimum of two days per month, or twenty-four days per annum, to each directorship, then seven of these will consume 168 days. The incidence of Board meetings, committee meetings and planning sessions will always be such that the logistics prevent him from working productively without breaks in his programme. He has less than three days per month for unavoidable gaps; just about enough for those sudden crises. Throw in weekends, forget about holidays, never mind the family, and still the most he could add is a sortie or two to the Middle East, where they work Sundays. The non-executive cannot do much useful work when there's no one else around. The law in France and Germany limits the number of Supervisory Board directorships one person can hold to eight and ten, respectively, and there are proposals that the numbers should be further reduced. Until quite recently the Chief Executive of one major German bank held over 100 directorships, and until quite recently the publishers of the *Directory of Directors*, a most fruitful reference, could still find one British Director with over 400 directorships. A gentle flip through its pages will indicate hundreds of other Directors with more than a dozen. Between these extremes stretch a lot of over-extended non-executives, who must worry from time to time that some of their companies might ask to see them again.

Not the acquiescent status symbol. In the words of Bruce Henderson, Chairman of Boston Consulting Group, one of the cleverest of the consulting houses: 'Most Chief Executives want little from Board members except public support, private philosophy, and no arguments and no initiatives. For these reasons their normal preference is for high status friends with high visibility and high responsibility which precludes much time spent or much interest in Board membership or responsibility'.

Not ever the acquiescent chum who has not been vetted by a committee of the Board to discover his potential contribution, who is clearly there to keep the Chairman or Chief Executive more comfortably in situ, and who demonstrates few relevant qualities other than dogged loyalty to his sponsor, and a friendly mien. Let the puppets hang in the strings already attached.

But maybe . . .

Maybe the technical specialist, but only if the company is so fundamentally technology-based that most items on the agenda need his presence; only if he and the Technical Director can keep from each other's throats; and only if it really is not possible to hire him as a technical consultant instead.

Maybe a major shareholder or his nominee. The shareholding Director, or nominee, has to keep at the front of his mind, always, that he is there to look after the interests of the company, not just those of himself or of his nominator. Even when it comes to voting on dividends. The majority can always vote him down, at least in a public company where that Director represents a minority, and has just one vote, anyway. Not so easy in a private company, where a large minority shareholder may come from another family, or from a feuding wing of the same family, and may introduce stresses into the Boardroom which have nothing whatever to do with the business in hand. Worse where the shareholder Director controls a majority of the shares, and consistently forgets that voting in the Boardroom is by number of hands, not by number of shares. Worst of all where the dominant shareholder Director controls only a minority, but where there is no counter-balancing minority, so that he can in practice run the show as though it was all his own. This occurs quite frequently in companies converted to 'public' status within the preceding decade or two, where the media, and almost everyone else, continue to call it 'his' company.

Given these common disadvantages, there is still much

value to be gained by an institutional shareholder requesting a Board to appoint its nominee when the institution concludes that the Board concerned is weak, or too in-bred. Company performance would be greatly improved if major institutions would only bother to do this more often – if they would just take that little bit more interest. The effort demanded from the institution is minimal. It has only to select the kind of man who would be most helpful to the Board concerned. After his appointment the man is 'the company's man', not in any way 'the institution's man'. He is on the Board to help the company, and thus the shareholders in total. If the institution has its own 'pool' of potential candidates, it can offer the Board two or three alternatives from which to make its selection. If the institution does not have such a pool, it can ask the Board to advertise. It can trigger action.

Maybe the nominee of the main lender. Particularly in a small or private company, which should be maintaining a close relationship with its bankers. The bank can suggest two or three names from its pool, or ask that the Board advertise, or point the Board in the direction of those organisations which assist in the recruitment of non-executives. Again, very little effort is demanded of the lender, beyond an active interest.

Maybe business-oriented academics, if they have already demonstrated their value as directors on other Boards. The proportion of US Boards which contain such academics is increasing. If the academic has not, yet, operated on a company Board, but some of the Directors know his style and believe it would fit, he can be tried out within the company on a 'consultancy' exercise. This will illustrate whether he can grip the realities as well as the theories. It will indicate whether he can develop the working respect of the senior executives, and prove to that critical gathering that he can contribute something of value. The Board can find that a lively, business-oriented academic can be more quick thinking than most of the Directors; can conceive more realistic alternatives to evaluate than anyone else; knows a lot more techniques to consider and questions to properly ask; sees at least the theoretical errors in cases proposed; speaks without prompting, and usually coherently. Directors are expected to 'ask searching questions'. It is a fact that most of them never do. The academic non-executive will.

Maybe the business or management consultant, but again only if he already has years of executive or non-executive directorship experience. The consultant whose career has been entirely within consulting houses may find it difficult to switch from giving advice into decision making or decision implementing. The argument most frequently raised against appointing consultants as non-executives is that they, too, are suppliers or services, who might either 'push' their services, or inhibit the company from engaging alternative consultants for specific assignments. This argument misses the point that when engaged as a non-executive the consultant joins the Board as a Director, not as a seller of specific services. The fact that he is a consultant by background simply defines the nature of his experience, and the likely style of his approach to the company's situation – the two criteria on which any potential Director should be judged.

The consultant who has already gained extensive management and directorship experience can be a most productive non-executive because:

- he has worked in a much wider variety of commercial and industrial environments than most executives cover during their careers;
- he is clinical in his approach to problems or opportunities;
- he may have experience of a wider range of functions than most executives;
- he has no inhibitions in telling home truths to top managements;
- he is likely to be the first, not the last, to suggest that some other consultant be brought in to handle a project which he and the executives conclude they cannot handle together. Which, as an aside, is a good argument for the one-man band consultant, rather than one from a traditional consulting house which has mouths to feed.

Walter Goldsmith of the Institute of Directors has stated that

'the non-executive is the company's own in-house management consultant.' All non-executives are indeed like consultants for part of their roles, so the experienced consultant
with Boardroom experience is a natural candidate for a non-
executive directorship. Most particularly in the small or
medium-sized company, where he can fill gaps in professional
or managerial knowledge without crossing chains of
command.

Maybe the full-time executive Director, Chairman or Chief
Executive from another company. But only if he can, is willing
to, and does, consistently meet the primary criterion for every
non-executive – a minimum average commitment to the
company of two days per month. It consumes one day per
month to prepare properly for a Board meeting, by studying
the papers, and then to attend it. It consumes another one day
per month, at least, to get around the company and really
understand its strengths, weaknesses, fantasies, foibles, and
high-flyers – including those who are still flying low down.

Appendix I illustrates that 88 per cent of large company
Boards in the USA contain non-executives who are full-time
executives elsewhere. The equivalent figures for the UK range
between 46 and 79 per cent, with evidence that a high proportion of these non-executives do not hold director-level positions in their employing companies. The amount of time
demanded, or at least tacitly accepted, from these people is
astonishingly small.

However great a person's experience and demonstrated
competence, if he does not spend enough time to get to know
the company of which he is a non-executive, he will not be
able to transfer that experience and competence to the solution of that company's problems and opportunities. His judgement can only be brought to bear on the papers tabled before
him, which only tell a small part of the story. To take an
everyday example, it does not help if the non-executive with
vast experience of production companies in the Far East votes
'go' on the new factory for Taiwan if the division or subsidiary
handling Taiwan is about to blow up from overwork, or alternatively has too little skill at the top of it to be able to control
the project, or if the Group Chief Executive supports the
project while everyone in the division down to the tea-ladies is

against it – but he knows nothing of all that because he has not been able to talk with the division lately. It does not help if the non-executive who has bought and sold more companies than most managers have had pay-slips votes 'no go' on an acquisition without which the division's product range will remain so incomplete that it will lose most of its markets in one year flat, and the humblest sales manager knows this – but he does not know this because he only read the relevant Board paper concerned on the train that morning. It does not help if the non-executive votes for a new Chief Executive who is supported by the two or three other Directors whom he does know quite well, but is strongly opposed by the several executive Directors whom he has never troubled to speak with (and by the tea-ladies and sales managers). It has not helped in those corporations which have gone under, or in countless others which manage to float along while the international competition goes sailing swiftly by.

The non-executive cannot be held culpable for poor managerial performance, but he can be held culpable for not having challenged and checked it. That is his function. It is most difficult to understand why so many men, who have achieved high reputations for their executive performance, have been so careless in their standards of non-executive performance.

There is a flurry of activity in the UK to promote the wider use of non-executives, aided by statements from institutions as influential as the Prudential Assurance that they would like to see at least three non-executives on the Boards of any companies in which they invest. The New York Stock Exchange requires that there be two in any company which seeks a listing, and a similar requirement could usefully be introduced by the London Stock Exchange. The reports which have triggered this promotional activity, the organisations behind it, and the several recruitment specialists pursuing it, all concentrate their attention almost exclusively on the recruitment of new non-executives from the catchment of full-time executives in other companies. This makes sense up to a point. Up to about half of the non-executive positions to be filled. It has to be remembered when recruiting that this is the catchment which has already demonstrated, in the UK and in the USA, that it is for the most part just too busy to be able to

commit the time necessary for the responsible performance of
the non-executive role. The role of the non-executive has been,
on average, performed poorly to date. It is not 'more of the
same' which is needed.

Maybe the hybrid or professional Director.

The hybrid Director

The first two hybrid Directors to receive widespread publicity
were appointed by BOC International. Primarily non-
executives, they were delegated a number of defined
functional roles which were intended to consume about a
quarter of their time.

At first sight the concept of the hybrid Director could seem
to run counter to the conventional wisdom that the non-
executive should maintain a strict separation from the
management, at least in larger Groups. At second sight, it is
only sensible that a Board delegate described part-time functions to those Directors best equipped to play them,
particularly if the Directors concerned would not be able to
play them full time, or if the roles themselves do not justify
engaging a full-time employee of the same calibre. Looked at
another way, if certain non-executives have expertise which
can be used to supplement the skills of the executives, why not
make use of it any way you can? There is no restriction on how
the Directors can be deployed, neither in law nor in sense.

While the first well-publicised example of the hybrid
concept was in a major international Group, the largest area
of potential application is naturally within smaller and
medium-sized companies. The smaller the company, the less
distinct the borderline between Board policy and executive
management. The more management detail comes up to the
Board, the more the Board itself operates as the top rung of
the management ladder, and the more there is to gain by
charging experienced non-executives to move into the
organisation for a spell to provide real assistance: for example
in

- helping to introduce new systems;
- describing new organisational structures;

- defining new review-and-report formats;
- building a planning mechanism;
- evaluating or even implementing a specific market assault;
- taking charge, in crisis, of a small new operation, or a set of territories.

This kind of contribution can be as productive to the company on a four to six days per month basis as if the men were full time. The 'pulse' of work triggered in the short period can require a further three weeks or so to progress and be developed by the management. After which the hybrid comes back in for another 'pulse' of input; withdraws; returns; and so on until the task is completed.

The difference between this role and the work of a wholly external consultant is that the Director concerned is part of the Board itself. He thus carries a significant additional level of enforced responsibility. Furthermore, he starts by knowing the company, and has no unproductive learning period. Among the thousands of companies which could profit greatly from engaging this kind of contribution, practically none is doing so to date.

The professional Director

The management writer, Peter Drucker, and Bruce Henderson of the Boston Consulting Group, have both argued the problem of composing an effective Boardroom through to the conclusion that the potentially most useful member of the Board is the professional Director, who sits on a maximum of five or six Boards and commits all his time and experience to this handful of roles.

> . . . the effective board member has to be a 'professional director'. Indeed board membership should be recognised as a full-time profession for a really first-rate man.
>
> PETER F. DRUCKER

The limitation on the total number of directorships is critical. It is to be hoped that the era of the man who sits on a dozen or more Boards is coming to a close. The catchment area for people who play the professional Director role, or who could and would play it responsibly, is currently limited only by the market's own limited awareness of this kind of potential non-executive contribution, or by its reluctance to engage it. Those who play the role share the common characteristic that they retain enough flexibility to switch into, and out of, a deeper commitment to any one of their companies, in step with how the companies' separate requirements shift in emphasis. They can slip into or out of a chairmanship, a temporary Chief Executive slot, or a part-time functional role to fill a gap or unravel a tangle.

None is the 'gifted amateur' of the folk-lore which surrounds the concept of the professional Director. The amateur, by definition, does it for fun. The professional Director lives by it. Which, for a start, strengthens his commitment and the force of his contribution.

The range of people playing this role has been slow to grow, in the past, because of the low level of non-executive fee rate which prevailed through to the late 1970s. These levels have lately risen sharply. The catchment area thus grows. When offered a few hundred pounds for the responsibilities of directorship, the non-executive will respond by giving the role what it is visibly worth. Hence the past predominance of cronies and dilettantes. Current American commentary suggests that the two-day-per-month non-executive should be paid 10 per cent of the twenty-day-per-month Chairman's fees. When the Chairman is a salaried employee, with cars, carpets, wall-to-wall secretaries, pensions and perquisites, then this percentage is about half too little.

In the Korn/Ferry survey of 1980 on a sample of 308 companies in the *Times 1000* (see Appendix I) the fee rate for non-executives in the largest companies averaged around £300 per day for an average of 16 days per annum committed. In the smaller companies in the sample, the fee rate averaged about £380 per day for the average of 13 days per annum committed. It might be concluded from this upside-down comparison that the smaller companies had expected a higher level of commitment when they settled their non-executives' annual fee, but did not get it.

By comparison, the traditional consulting houses are invoicing their clients at a similar per diem for the services of middle-range consultants, while the haute consulting houses and major accounting firms are charging very much higher rates for senior men. The professional Director working for, say, four companies at an average of four 'chargeable' days per month – or two companies at four days and four companies at two days – at £300 per day, will gross £57,600 per annum if he has no gaps in his programme. (He will in fact always have gaps, often big ones.) The figure of £57,600 is what it costs a company to employ an executive on a salary of £28,800, using the normally accepted multiplier of 2. Published data has shown that the executive Director in medium-sized to large public companies had an average salary of about £28,000 in 1980.

Companies do handsomely on these calculations, having on tap an experienced man with director-level responsibility, who can be switched on and off at less cost than a senior executive, and without any of the complications of the Employment Acts. The professional Director can also do well, if he can plug most of his gaps. He has his own heavy overheads, but these are certainly less than half of his gross income.

It is conventional wisdom that the non-executive should be financially independent, and thus able to wield his ultimate weapon, resignation, without fear of damaging his personal situation. The rather puritanical implication has been that the fees are not important to him. Certainly the non-executive must not be so dependent on any one company's fees that he dares not resign from its Board when the company is behaving in a way which he cannot accept and cannot amend. But if an employee is motivated by the level of remuneration for his efforts, why not also the non-executive? Any Director will inevitably, if subconsciously, gear the depth of his involvement to the value which he can see the company places on his services. Of course 'value' is directly correlated with '£'. A useful rule-of-thumb for a Board about to appoint a non-executive would be to:

- take the salary of the highest paid Director – you want a non-executive who is as good as that Director;
- multiply it by 2 (the multiplier which many City companies use for their budgeting is 2.25);
- divide it by 200 (there being only 200 productive days in

a year, and each non-executive day should be packed and productive);

— multiply the figure obtained by the number of full days per annum which it has been agreed the non-executive will contribute to the company. This gives the annual fee rate.

For example, when the Chief Executive is the highest paid Director and has an annual salary of £30,000, costing his company £60,000 gross, the two-day-per-month non-executive receives a per diem of £300, or £7,200 for the time he commits. The smaller company, with a less well-salaried Chief Executive, will have to adjust these figures a little to attract the right calibre of men, but it is hoped that the guidelines will be helpful in stiffening their resolve to settle for nothing less than the right calibre, and the right extent of commitment. Anything less on either count will mean money down the drain.

The concept of the professional Director runs counter to the thinking of virtually all the organisations currently concerned with locating non-executives for companies which want them. One of them has put this succinctly by saying that the non-executive needs also to have 'an executive power base'. Why a non-executive should need a 'power base' is far from clear. Anyone playing the professional Director role, sensibly, will have had one or several such power bases during his executive career. The non-executive works inside the Board; he is not an ornament to impress the world outside the Board. Chapter 9 examines ways of getting round this severely limiting approach to the recruitment of non-executives, but it is worth summarising a few of the negative effects which it produces.

Firstly, the Board deprives itself of, or is deprived of, the opportunity to consider a great variety of available experience. Secondly, the Board limits its vision to those who may not be able to give it enough time. Thirdly, the Board's catchment area includes only those executives whose companies will allow them to be non-executives elsewhere. Fourthly, because this so severely trims the catchment area of experienced executive Directors, the Board may be offered men who hold senior executive positions elsewhere, but do not have senior directorship experience. (Half of the UK non-executives who are executives in other companies already fall into this category – see Appendix I.) The non-executive should be a contributor, not a learner. Fifthly, when a company does release men to be non-executives in other companies it could be tempted to release those who have reached their limits as executives, and really do have time on their hands – for the wrong reasons. The receiving company, or for that matter the recruiting organisation, will have little means of identifying whether they are handling a high-flyer who is being lent out to spread his wings a little, or the very opposite – unless age is an indicator.

It is useful to turn to American experience with non-executives, because the bulk of their Boardrooms are made up of part-time Directors. The majority of these are full-time executives or Chief Executive Officers in other companies, and in all public commentary in the USA on the role of the non-executive the problem of inadequate time commitment comes at the top of the list of complaints.

The *Harvard Business Review* of May–June 1976 published an article by Joseph W. Barr, himself a professional Director on several Boards, which summarised a survey of opinion from 160 large companies on the question of using 'professional Directors' instead of the existing categories, whose limited contribution was the cause of the public commentary and complaint. The survey found that there was much support for the concept. Those objections which were raised by some respondents could be grouped into the following:

1　A dislike of the term 'professional Director'.
2　A belief that the Chief Executive Officer of another company could still contribute, despite the time problem.
3　A concern that the professional Director might blur the lines between management and the supervision of management by not being able to keep his hands off day-to-day operations.
4　That the professional Director would want his own staff.
5　That the extra remuneration paid to the professional Director might impair his independence.

6   That 'We wish we didn't have any outsider Directors, especially no professional Directors'.

The last comment says it all. But taking the objections one by one:

1   The term used naturally matters little, and most alternatives would raise equal objections.

2   If Chief Executive Officers acting as non-executives in other companies were contributing well enough, then there would be no concern about the performance of Boards in the USA and the UK. But concern is considerable, and well-founded. In addition, there is already widespread complaint about the high proportion of interlocking directorships, which result when company *A* lends one of its executives to company *B* as a non-executive, and receives back from company *B* one of their men to be one of its own non-executives. The term 'incest' has been used to describe the process. There have been anti-trust suits regarding such interlocking directorships, and the relationship between Directors on the Boards of financial institutions has come under particular scrutiny. One is reminded of the Whitley Study data on the City of London (see Chapter 2). Precisely the same situation could develop in UK industry if the catchment area for recruiting non-executives is restricted largely to full-time executives.

3   The role of the non-executive can be defined to include as little or as much involvement with management as the Board sees fit. The outsider who cannot keep his hands off day-to-day operations when told to do so can be removed.

4   The professional Director would make use of the company's existing staff, for the provision of existing data, for secretarial services when necessary, or for any other ad hoc requirement. There is no reason why he should need to add to the company's numbers in any way.

5   The professional Director who operates on a small

number of Boards would not be dependent on any one of them.

6   Few executives like to have non-executives sniffing around, if they have anything which they do not want to be seen, or which embarrasses them. The executive who is working well, has ideas to contribute, and is looking for a way up the corporate ladder will be only too glad to expose his activities and suggestions to an independent outsider who is willing and able to bring them to the Board's attention. This is one of the main reasons for having non-executives sniffing around. The problem is that the prevailing style of non-executive on either side of the Atlantic goes on demonstrating that he does not have, or give, the time to perform that potentially productive function at all.

Late in 1979, when there was much Press commentary on the role of the non-executive in the UK, Kenneth Fleet, of *Financial Weekly*, castigated the recruitment of non-executives from 'the ranks of generals, admirals, corporate has-beens, "professional" non-executives, thrusters, amateurs and cranks' on the basis that 'however clever such men may be, they can contribute very little of real value because their time and interests are too divided'. The same commentary supported the recruitment of non-executives from the ranks of full-time executives, and only from such ranks, and rounded off the article with further castigation of the professional Director with 'six, ten or twenty' different directorships. This neatly illustrates the confusion on the role of the non-executive which continues to delay their fuller and more responsible deployment through companies of all shapes and sizes which need them.

Firstly, there is a whole world of difference between six directorships and twenty. Six can be the ideal number. Twenty can be a bad joke. Secondly, the full-time executive has less time available than the professional Director, not more. Thirdly, the full-time executive's interests are more divided, not less, than those of the professional Director, who does not have a one-company career to protect; is not interrupted every nine minutes; sits on fewer Boards than the senior executive Director in a Group.

Every one of the scores of intelligent and well-intentioned US and UK commentaries on the past failures of the non-executive which has appeared in print in the last decade, Mr Fleet's article included, has focused on the problem of the time needed by the non-executive to play his role well and responsibly.

The Board makes its own final decision when appointing men to its number. On the evidence, its very first question to all candidates must be whether or not the people considered really can, and really will, provide the level of commitment and contribution which the company requires. If there is the slightest doubt on this, then the Board must look elsewhere. Is the company worth at least two days a month, or not?

Actions for non-executives

A prospective non-executive should:

1   Determine if the company is recruiting seriously and methodically. If it has advertised, if he first meets a committee of three to four Board members, and if the committee can succinctly describe the company's situation, and what it requires from the new non-executive, then it probably is. If it has not advertised, if he meets only one Director, and if he has difficulty in unearthing details of the company's situation, or why it is looking for a non-executive, then it certainly is not. If it cannot recruit well, then it probably cannot do a lot of other things very well either.

2   Query the committee of Directors regarding the company:

its shareholders, and the relations between them, if a private company;

its business, markets and competition;

its key problems and opportunities, both current and anticipated;

its performance and financial situation, as evidenced by current and recent past accounts presented by the committee.

3 Determine the composition of the Board and senior management, and the structure of the company as a whole:

Who does what, how well?

Is the Chairman also Chief Executive, and does he intend to remain so? Angus Murray, whose performance as a non-executive of Newman Industries represented a milestone in the development of responsible directorship, has stated that he would not join a Board where the Chairman remains the Chief Executive.

Does the Chief Executive appear to lead or dominate?

Does the Finance Director have at his fingertips all the opinions and data which he seeks? Particularly a sound cash flow forecast? If not, it could be that the data presented are misleading, or wrong.

Are there other non-executives, and if not, are there plans to recruit others? Of what kind, and when? If the concept of a non-executive is new to that Boardroom it can be good policy to engage just one to begin with, but on the understanding that, once the credibility of the concept has been established in the company, there will be others. One man alone can find it difficult to force through effective change. He risks getting classified as a 'boat rocker' if it is always just him who says that change, |of whatever kind, is needed, and this can delay or destroy the executives' acceptance of the value of non-executive contribution.

4 Meet all the Directors and, if reasonably possible, a number of the senior managers just below the Board. Speak freely with them; seek to elicit gently what concerns them most about the company, and about his possible appointment to its Board.

5 Determine whether he can fit in. The term 'chemistry' is often used. In fact chemistry is all about the production of new chemicals, which

implies change to the original mix, not a comfortable maintenance of the status quo. As long as the 'chemistry' will not lead to constant explosions, it should be judged solely on the likely changes it will induce, not on miscibility.

6   Ensure that what he is expected to contribute is understood and accepted by the Board as a whole.

7   If all parties still remain interested, but if the prospective non-executive is not happy with the accuracy or reality of the performance data presented to him, he should consider asking for a meeting with the company's auditors or bankers. At this stage, any such discussions must be handled with utmost diplomacy, but if he cannot exercise diplomacy outside the Boardroom then he is not going to be very effective inside it either.

8   Agree on the content and extent of information which will be provided to him as a routine, and that he will obtain a comprehensive initial induction into the company on appointment.

9   Agree a minimum and maximum length of appointment, normally at least two years and at most five years. The company should have changed so much in five years that it then needs a quite different mix in the Boardroom. He may still be useful after that period, but the question should be formally reviewed, not neglected by default.

10   Agree a time commitment and a fee rate. If the Board wants less than an average of two days per month, it does not want enough. If he cannot give at least two days per month, he cannot give enough.

Once he has joined the Board, he should:

11   Ensure he receives the agreed induction. Otherwise everyone else will forget about it.

12   Ensure he receives the agreed information in the agreed format, and to a regular timetable.

13   Ensure that he maintains contact with all the Directors, and with other key executives below the Board. He must temper his comments and thinking

in the Boardroom with his direct knowledge of the people involved.

14 Ensure he has an annual review of his role and performance with the Chairman.

15 Ask for items to be placed on the agenda if he feels key issues are being overlooked, or deliberately suppressed, never simply accepting what is put before him.

16 Ensure that Board reviews of performance go beyond just expressing satisfaction or concern; that they lead to minuted decisions regarding future action by the management.

17 Ensure that the Board looks forwards as well as backwards; not just forwards through the budgeted year, but into the longer-term plan period also.

18 Participate to an agreed extent in the planning process. This may mean attending some long weekend sessions with senior executives – which can be one of the very best ways of getting to know the company's businesses, staff, strengths and weaknesses.

19 Accept specifically delegated projects where he is the best placed to carry them out. Besides thus helping the company, he may develop a better 'feel' for the company's real situation in its external environment through such projects. Often the company's true competitive position is quite different from what the executives believe, and from what is consequently reported in the Boardroom.

20 Accept directorships in Divisional or Subsidiary Boards if he can be of assistance to those companies also, and if he feels he can thereby improve the quality of the linkages through the company from top to bottom.

21 Ensure he gives the time agreed; at least two days per month, and more in times of crisis. This means that he can responsibly perform only seven such roles as a professional Director, or one if employed full-time elsewhere.

22 Speak out if the Board is observed to be failing:

    to define policies and objectives, or maintain
    planning and budgeting routines;

    to deploy and measure returns on resources;

    to properly define management's authority, or
    monitor its performance;

    to maintain, and use critically, a sound financial
    reporting system;

    to maintain effective communication and
    participation, company wide;

    to monitor its own performance as a Board; or

    to keep within both the letter and the spirit of all
    the laws.

Describe how to improve the Board's performance, and if judged necessary, have this minuted. Ensure that corrective action is actually carried out.

23   Remember always that the Board has to act for the benefit of the company as a whole, and that the Directors are the agents of the company, not of the shareholders or of any other specific interests, least of all their own.

24   Remember in crisis that his weapons include talking with the company's auditors and bankers and, in the final extreme, with the shareholders. In private companies the main shareholders may be within the Board, so threatened approach to the auditors or bankers may stimulate a more responsible reaction.

25   Remember that, while resignation is his last weapon, it can often harm the company rather than help it, particularly if a well-publicised resignation is not accompanied by a clear statement of the reasons why he felt compelled to resign. Further, that resignation may remove from the Board the only person who is able to help it at all.

Employee representation

Those who argue for the appointment of union Directors or worker Directors to controlling Boards in the UK do so on the basis that without such specialist directors there is a continuing risk that the Board may ride roughshod over the interests of the employees – not on the basis that their presence will improve competitive business decision making.

Those who argue against, do so on one or more of the bases that:

- established trade unions are already well placed to root out both collective or individual abuses and to exact remedies where the company has been at fault. Further, that this wholly proper position of power is already itself too often improperly abused;
- the great majority of trade unions themselves do not want to see the introduction of employee Directors in the UK, preferring to manoeuvre or do battle, as they judge fit, outside the Boardroom. On this they differ markedly from the Trades Union Congress;
- employee representation has not helped to build better businesses where it has been applied, and is already creating divisive tensions where it has been over applied. Witness the saga in 1980 of Mannesmann and the Free Democrats versus the Union I.G.Metall and the Social Democrats in West Germany, a country whose government consists of a coalition between the same Free Democrats and Social Democrats; a country where disruptive industrial action has rarely been taken for any reason, and seldom before 1980 for purely political reasons;
- the 'them' who want it, as opposed to the 'us' who do not, still cannot make up their own minds as to whether such Directors should be employees or union officials. Or from which union. (British Steel has to grapple with 28 unions.) And that half the workforce is not a member of any one of those unions;
- all the executive Directors are employees, too, and even that tiny fraction which might ride roughshod over the workforce, given the chance, has learned the hard way that it will not be given the chance.

In view of the distance between the two arguments, various alternatives have been suggested to seek to bridge the gap.

The Industrial Society, for example, whose own constitution embodies a cooperation between unions and industrial managements, has long promoted the concept that the annual report of a company should name two of the Directors as representing the employees, and should record that both of them have the employees' confidence. This implies that steps would need to be taken to confirm, internally, that such confidence in the two Directors does in fact exist. This process could be hedged about with all kinds of opportunity for sabotage, character assassination, filibustering, or just plain stubbornness, and the exercise might not be able to be conducted without internal harm.

Another alternative would require the TUC, on behalf of its constituent unions, to build up a very large cadre of 'their' men who could be offered to Boards, in much the same way that union-oriented nominees are offered to industrial tribunals. While the accumulation of business understanding, over a period of years, could most usefully result in guiding future union behaviour, this concept would not be workable if the unions and the TUC were not prepared to support it, exclusively, and take on the amount of work it would involve. But to any responsible Director the subject is quite simply irrelevant. The law itself now quite clearly says all that needs saying (Companies Act, 1980, Part IV, s. 46):

(1) The matters to which the directors of a company are to have regard in the performance of their functions shall include the interests of the company's employees in general as well as the interests of its members.

(2) Accordingly, the duty imposed by subsection (1) above on the directors of a company is owed by them to the company (and the company alone) and is enforceable in the same way as any other fiduciary duty owed to a company by its directors.

True, under English law only those to whom a duty is owed can sue in respect of a wrong done by another person, and it has already been argued by some company lawyers that only the company, through one of its members, i.e. shareholders, can take legal action to force the Directors to undertake their obligations to the employees. But the employee can be a shareholder, or can lobby a shareholder. Or the courts may take the view that the employee does not need to be a member to take an action, given the very clear intention of this legislation. The legal niceties matter little. The Board which operates in disregard of the intention of this law will find itself open to public chastisement of a kind far more effective than court action.

The concept of worker Directors and union Directors has been tried in the UK. The Post Office experimented with seven such Directors on its Board for two years, and gave it up. No one has been reported to date as having said that the experiment achieved anything that could not have been achieved by appointing any group of seven sensible people. On the contrary, some of the Post Office Directors have gone on record as saying that the presence of identifiably separate interests on the Board had clogged up the proceedings.

The Post Office Board had also contained five 'consumer' Directors during the same period. No one can pretend that service to the consumer has improved as a result of the experiment. During the period of the experiment such service demonstrably worsened. The Post Office survived only because of its monopoly status. One of the specialist Directors stated that: 'the Board has never been a success and it never could be'. This is not too surprising when one takes into account that the Board concerned contained a total of 19 Directors, 12 of them representing specialised interests, none of which had anything to do with the basic business of providing postal and telecommunication services, efficiently.

Stripped to its bones of political or emotive irrelevancies, the concept of employee-representing Directors can be seen to be fundamentally absurd. In all human relationships, just as in all animal relationships, there are territorial boundaries. When animals cross boundaries, they fight. Humans have developed two options; to cross a boundary and make war, or to cross a boundary in order to cooperate. But this does not eliminate the fact that the interest groups still exist, behind their boundaries.

The overriding responsibility and objective of the Board, also in law, is the interest of the company as a whole. Interest groups have, by definition, another overriding objective. That is why the boundaries of any interest group can come up to, but not into, the boundaries of the Boardroom. That is why there should be no specialist interests represented on any Board.

In the People's Republic of China a crack has appeared in the structure of communist ownership of all the means of production and distribution. In the Jindi People's Commune in Shandong Province a new joint-stock company has been formed. It is the first capitalist venture in China since the revolution. The company is run by the stockholders' representatives. There are no employee representatives; no union Directors, no worker Directors.

In little of the debate on this debilitating subject has it been highlighted that in West Germany, on whose laws the original proposals for union Directors and worker Directors were modelled, the law also differs from that of the UK in that: collective agreements are binding on all parties; unions and their officials enjoy no legal immunities; unions must be independent of political parties, and closed shops are illegal.

In none of the debates has it been suggested, even with tongue in cheek, that union or worker representation on Boards should be matched by Directors and managers having seats at all the most important union meetings, and that Directors and managers should be empowered, by law, to influence union policy making. That concept is equally absurd. But not more so.

7 External responsibilities

The Board bears responsibilities to

- the law at large;
- the customer;
- the community, through the law;
- the shareholders;
- the creditors and lenders.

Its relationships with the first three categories were considered in Chapter 3. Which brings us to . . .

The shareholders

The shareholders do not own the company or the assets. They own shares, which gives them certain rights. The company only belongs to them, in a formal sense, at time of dissolution, and even then they come last in the list of interested parties.

Most Directors will be surprised that their duty is not to the shareholders, but to the company as an entity. This has always been so, though never so clearly expressed as in s.46 of the Companies Act 1980. Most shareholders will be equally surprised, even affronted. Yet the realities, quite apart from the legalities, are that in all but the smallest private companies, the shareholders

- are numerous;
- can include little old ladies and mighty institutions;
- can have quite different prime interests, such as short-term dividends versus long-term capital gains; and
- can therefore only be collectively served by a Board

which focuses its attention exclusively on the survival and prosperity of the company.

In large public Groups, where the majority of the shares are owned by a variety of institutional investors, the objectives and interests of one institution, in any one year, can differ from those of another – or from its own interests in any other year. One may have bought in at £1 per share, and be satisfied by a quite different level of return than another institution which purchased at £2.

Even in the small or new private company, where the members may have staked their last penny on that investment, the Board can only protect their combined interests by first ensuring the survival and prosperity of the company as a whole.

The only time when the Board must focus on the shareholders' interests, specifically, is when the company is subject to a takeover bid. Here ownership of shares may change hands at a collectively determined price. Here the existing owners of the shares must be given clear details of all the options open to them at a point of discontinuity in the company's history. They may make different judgements on what to do with their shares, dependent, perhaps, on the different prices at which they bought into the company – so even then the Board can only place them 'equal first'.

The Board owes the shareholders, specifically, just four additional duties:

  – to register share transfers;
  – to present the annual general meeting with a balance sheet and profit and loss account, together with the Directors' and Chairman's reports;
  – to call general meetings, whether annual or extraordinary, within the required timetables; and
  – to ensure that minorities are treated equally, and without 'unreasonable prejudice'.

The shareholder can decide to treat his shareholding like a lottery ticket, or to keep close to the workings of the company. The choice is his. To appoint or remove Directors; to approve accounts; to appoint auditors; to alter the objects of a company's operations in its Memorandum, or to alter the Articles under which the Directors operate – the power is his. To request the Department of Trade to investigate the company; to petition the court for a compulsory winding up of the company if it has failed, or if the Articles have not been complied with, or if the Directors have acted illegally – the power is also his.

Following the Prudential Assurance *v*. Newman Industries judgement in 1980, the power of the shareholder has been strengthened by making it more practicable to bring claims against Directors for breach of duty. In the US such claims are very common. In the UK, it might be argued, they are not yet common enough. In the US the Directors can face action from the shareholders for resisting a takeover bid which could have increased the value of their shares; for making a bad acquisition which does not produce the anticipated returns, and most acquisitions do not; for investing too much in research and development for nebulous new products; for doing too little research and development and falling behind the market . . .

In the UK the quiescence of many a Board may simply reflect the acquiescence of the average shareholder to its level of performance. One of the large institutional shareholders stated recently the opinion, in mid-recession to boot, that of the several hundred companies in which it invested, less than two dozen caused it concern. The Governor of the Bank of England stated in 1978 that 'Institutional shareholders should take trouble to ensure that Directors of companies in which they have important investments are doing a good job. If they are doubtful or uneasy, they should ask for explanations and expect to receive them . . . if in the end they are dissatisfied, they should, individually or collectively, take steps to change the composition of the Board'.

While the shareholder cannot alter a decision made by the Board (such as buying a property, or fixing a maximum level of dividend), and cannot view the minutes of the Board meetings, he does have in his hands the one power which most directly affects the performance of any company, of any shape or size – the power 'to change the composition of the Board'.

It can therefore be argued that the shareholder's responsibility to the company is far greater than the Board's responsibilities to the shareholders.

Creditors and lenders

The trade creditor is the least protected component in the trading process. When a company is liquidated, he comes second from last in the queue, followed only by the limited liability shareholders, and preceded by:

- receivership fees and fixed charges (which means 'bankers');
- preferential creditors, such as PAYE, VAT, rates, other taxes, wages and salaries; and
- floating charges (which also means 'bankers').

In the run-up to collapse and liquidation he certainly has access via Companies House, bankers and credit reference organisations to the same basic categories of information on the company's financial situation as available to shareholders, but it is always older and thinner. He does not have the shareholder's ability to question the Board on the anticipated future financial situation, nor to pressure the Board to carry out improvements. He has to judge the limit to which he will risk supplying the company with goods or services not paid for COD, and there is no limitation to his risk beyond that individual judgement. In times of recession he will commonly extend the size of his collected risks to the point of insomnia, just to keep his works in motion. And at precisely the same times the abuse of the trade creditor by his customers is similarly extended.

The prime responsibility of the company to the creditor is to pay his invoices to time. Unreasonable extension of the payment period constitutes a breach of contract. The smaller supplier can seldom afford to sue a larger customer, and thus often submits to mistreatment when he is himself at his weakest. When a company breaches an external responsibility by failing to pay its creditors to time, it is also causing itself internal harm. When a company begins to rely on breaking the rules, it begins to lose track of, and control of, its real situation.

The writer was once involved in assisting a company fast approaching collapse. One of the first actions was, naturally, to phase the debtors and tighten the chase for cash. Another action was to compile an accurate record of its overdue creditors. By the time the company was able to do this, it had gone bust. The Board had run away from their business responsibilities. Their business had run away from them.

Yet in times of trouble the Board will normally acquiesce in the stretching of payment periods. This can be the worst of decisions, or of matters left undecided. It can increase the company's problems rather than alleviate them. Elastic payment periods get noticed; creditors ring around; rumours begin; customers hear them, and business falls away – just when it is most needed. The 'old faithful' repeat orders are withheld; the faithful old supplier says 'enough'; alternative suppliers hesitate.

The Board would be wise to insist, in good times and bad, that the same firmness is applied to meeting creditors' invoices as is applied, or should be applied daily, to the collection of debtors due. And it should not differentiate between categories of creditor. If the company can only survive by a methodical breach of supply contracts, then it not only does not deserve to survive, but it assuredly will not survive for long.

The lenders, primarily the clearing banks in the UK, are in a stronger position. They may require fixed charges, or fixed and floating charges, on the company's assets. The value of the assets charged can greatly exceed the total amount which has been lent. Then, as a secured creditor, the bank can put in a receiver when the company becomes insolvent. Contrary to popular belief, a company does not have to cease trading when its liabilities exceed its assets. It has to cease trading when the Directors judge they can no longer be sure of meeting credit when it falls due. Any new credit taken after a company becomes insolvent can become the personal liability of the Director who took it. The decision on whether new credit can be met depends on whether or not the bank will extend the overdraft; given time, tighter (or new) management, closure of loss makers and selective sales of assets, the company might be able to trade out of an assets deficiency. In practice, therefore, it is often the bank's decision about the overdraft, not the Board's decision, which determines whether or not a company goes into receivership.

Sometimes the decision is clear cut. The company, on all the evidence carefully and responsibly collected, has no chance, or almost no chance, of ever trading out of trouble; the excess of liabilities over assets will continue to grow. Sometimes it is a question of how long the bank will 'stick with it'; it does, after all, receive interest on the overdraft. The bank cannot be blamed for basing at least part of its decision on how close the 'distressed sale' value of the assets lies to the total amount which would have to be lent. It can, on the other hand, quite often be blamed for watching the company's situation slip steadily over a long period of time, without pressing the Board to make changes. The bank knows, better than anyone, that the process of receivership can drain large sums away from what would otherwise be available to other creditors:

- receivership fees are steep;
- distressed sales can bring below-book prices;
- 'going concern' parts of the company lose customers, and their own potential sale price reduces;
- some debtors begin to find good reasons why they should not pay.

The Board has a responsibility to its bankers to ensure that the financial or other information which it provides when requesting loan or overdraft facilities is as accurate as the Board can make it. But this also places a responsibility on the bankers. When a Board requests extended facilities because of trading or other difficulties, the bank quite properly requires that it subsequently receive regular data from the company in balance sheet and profit and loss formats, together with cash flow forecasts. It may request to receive these monthly. This puts into the bank's hands fresher and fuller data than are available to shareholders. The bank inevitably becomes close to the Board. It can sense the Board's weaknesses. At least it should be able to, if the bank manager is competent. It can recommend changes. It can press for changes, particularly to the composition of the Board.

Given the bank's singular ability to protect its own position, and given the extent of the information it can properly require, it can be argued that from the first moment that trouble is detected, the bank's responsibility to the interests of the company, which includes the interests of the employees and of the other creditors, is as real as the Board's responsibility to the bank.

8 Company collapse

Receivership is the ultimate sanction for bad management, which means for bad Boards. Luck rarely comes into it. Analyses of collapsed companies by accounting firms which handle numerous insolvencies reveal a common pattern of weaknesses and mistakes, and misfortune is seldom a factor.

Certainly a recession adds stresses which are not in the Board's power to control, but to which it must react, however cold-bloodedly. Certainly the most taut management disciplines and Board monitoring are needed to counteract an insanely high cost of borrowing; the continuation of locally high inflation; the growing competition from developing countries; the continued impoverishment of countries developing and developed, to the exclusive benefit of an astonishingly small number of people who happened to pitch their tents on top of oil. Certainly the rate of corporate insolvency will grow apace. It will always exceed the published data, which does not include subsidiaries kept alive by internal funding long after they are dead, nor bankrupt businesses interchanged between Groups, nor such businesses which are quietly dissolved by their parent.

Directors are seldom aware that it is against the law to continue to trade when technically insolvent, that is, when unable to meet credit when it falls due. Or that they risk personal liability for credit taken during the period of insolvency. They may become aware, the uncomfortable way. The threat of insolvency is no longer confined to small or medium-sized companies. Dr Richard Taffler of Performance Analysis Services Ltd, a lecturer at the City University Business School, has demonstrated by computer modelling techniques that at mid-1980 110 of the top 850 quoted manufacturing companies analysed by PAS were at risk, and that by the end of 1980 the

140

figure would be well over 150. Of the 200 companies at the bottom of the sample of 850, Dr Taffler believes from the evidence that the managements of fully 140 are 'uncertain what to do, are taking inappropriate action or no action, or are unaware of the danger signs. . . . What's frightening is the number of companies going down that haven't been spotted'. Given that Dr Taffler used these techniques to forecast the crises at Bond Worth, Staflex, Dunbee-Combex-Marx and other companies before the City analysts managed to, then these managements and their Boards have received fair warning.

Rates of change increase with time, be they changes in markets, technologies or competitive methods, and this leaves Boards with progressively less time to react to declining situations. The detailed factors which lie behind company collapse, and to which Boards must therefore apply priority attention, have been recorded by a major international accounting firm as follows.

Causes and symptoms in 20 company failures

Bad management   20

High gearing	11
No financial projections	9
Poor costing	8
Overtrading	7
Not reading economic signposts	6
Excessive overheads	6
Not selling production	6
Selling too cheap	5
Excessive research and development	5
Extravagance	4
Sales mix problems	4
Raw material shortage	3
Labour shortage	2
Overstocking	2
Engineering problems	2
Poor production planning	2
Fixed price contracts	1

Bad luck	1
Failure of bankers	1
Fraud	1

But these are just the symptoms. Behind them lie causes. In the words of the accounting firm: 'It's odd how the public at large often see the collapse of a company as being a financial failure, but often this represents a misunderstanding of the position. True, collapse does not often occur until the company runs out of money, but the process of running out of money is often a mere symptom of the disease which has already taken hold'.

In their conclusion, the defects which place the business at risk are described as one or more of the following:

1   An autocratic Chief Executive who heeds no advice and flies the business 'by the seat of his pants'. He often collects people around him who do not argue with him because those that do argue do not stay.

2   Imbalanced skills. Perhaps too many engineers as was commented on in the case of Rolls-Royce. Perhaps a failure of a growing business to recognise that people do not always grow with the job.

3   Over-confidence, manifesting itself in a failure to project forward the down side of projects or business decisions as well as the up side. Failure to appreciate the consequence for the business if the project goes wrong.

4   An absence of budget appraisal. No profit plan or cash flow plan prepared conscientiously and logically.

5   A failure to apply budgetary control. Budgets which go straight into the bottom drawer and are not used as a plan of action for developing and controlling the business, much as an engineer might use a blue-print.

6   A failure to use management information. Management refusing to believe the information which is produced, or ignoring it, or both. You will know the

ploys used in meetings to discredit information when the message it conveys is unpalatable.

7 A lack of toughness in dealing with third parties. Often found in sales-oriented companies where people will concede any point in order to clinch a sale, and will then use the fear of upsetting the customer as a reason for not collecting the debt when due.

8 A failure to respond to change until it overwhelms them.

Also in their conclusion, these defects are characteristically followed by mistakes which expose the underlying defects, and which include:

1 The creation of contingent liabilities. Often companies, particularly companies within Groups, find themselves giving guarantees with potential liabilities substantially in excess of the company's ability to meet the claim under the guarantee without endangering their own solvency.

2 Incorrect gearing. A complex issue . . . it may result from over-rapid growth of borrowed funds . . . the cash generated from trading being more than absorbed in cash-hungry projects which generate little cash return in the short term, necessitating increased borrowing.

3 Over-trading. When turnover rises at a greater rate than the cash flow generated from trading there is a need to finance the increased turnover.

4 Entering into major contracts, the consequences of which are not fully comprehended. In some respects this is a lack of business discipline, and it may also reflect an unwillingness to spend a few pounds on some professional advice.

5 Major new projects. Taking on projects which are substantial in size in relation to the existing business, in fields where the company's management has little or no expertise, without allowing for the down side, or without taking steps to control the project and isolate it from the rest of the business.

These mistakes then characteristically lead into the third stage of financial malaise and progressive collapse, which includes the sequence of:

- failure to react to the warning signs;
- low profitability or loss making;
- adverse cash flow;
- extended credit taken from suppliers;
- adverse gearing, where there develops an over dependence on lenders as against the company's own resources;
- increasing losses as the situation deteriorates;
- with the business tumbling out of control, the management becomes totally absorbed in plugging gaps and staving off creditors in order to survive until the following day.

Each initial defect in the above summary is visible to a Board which is alive to its responsibilities. If the Board is wholly executive, or if its non-executives are of the one-day-per-month variety, then the defects will often go unchallenged until it is too late to challenge or change. But the defects will be visible. The onus lies on any Director who sees them to expose his concern, and to require management action. The executive Director may do this once or twice, but will seldom keep at it long enough for improvement to be finally effected; it feels too much like destroying the solidarity of the team, and it certainly means upsetting his boss.

The weight falls on the non-executives. They have no boss except the Board. Their team is the Board. The Board as a whole is always responsible.

These characteristics of companies which fail provide a practical checklist against which the responsible Board can measure its own company's situation. They are the conclusions of one major international accounting firm, which has viewed company collapse from the inside.

Strikingly similar conclusions were reached by an 'outside' study of a number of failed companies published in *Corporate Collapse* by John Argenti (McGraw-Hill 1976). This study also found that fraud or bad luck were insignificant factors, but that there was always one or more of six basic defects:

1   One-man rule. A Chief Executive who dominated
    rather than led. The difference between a successful,
    dominant leader and an unsuccessful autocrat could
    be determined by other, more visible features of the
    company.

2   A non-participating Board. Not just non-executives
    who did not know the company's true situation, but
    also executives who awoke only when their
    specialised function was under discussion. Note here
    the similarity with bad cabinets. Richard Crossman
    wrote in his diaries that 'We came [to Cabinet meet-
    ings] briefed by our Departments to fight for our
    Departmental budgets, not as Cabinet Ministers with
    a Cabinet view'. A passive Board enables the autocrat
    to suppress discussion, or to prevent controversy
    coming to the Board at all.

3   An unbalanced top team, e.g. where all the Directors
    are engineers. 'If the Board does not contain a wide
    spectrum of skills then the chances of some new
    threat appearing but going unnoticed is severely
    increased'.

4   Lack of management depth.

5   Weak finance function, especially at the very top.
    John Argenti plays down this feature in comparison
    with others, though the writer has seen corporate
    death result from this specific defect.

6   A combined Chairman/Chief Executive. Not all the
    participants in Argenti's study agreed that this was a
    basic defect. But it must be self-evident that it is one
    where any of the other defects also appear.

Again, all these defects are visible to the Board which is alive
to its responsibilities. Where the Board is not sufficiently alive,
a number of management weaknesses will arise, which the
Argenti study recorded as:

1   Poor accounting information. Poor comparison of 1–5
    year budgets against actual performance, i.e. poor
    budgetary control; poor costing systems; inadequate
    cash flow forecasting. Top managers know the
    company is failing, but the lack of an adequate

system of information means they can keep quiet, and the Board does not detect the growing problem.

2   Inadequate response to change, whether competitive, political, social, economic or technological. Sometimes external constraints were found to have hindered the company's ability to respond freely to change, e.g. the constraint not to increase prices; not to build a pipeline or factory; not to make a merger; or not to do anything very dramatic at all, for example as a result of trade union opposition. This led to . . .

3   Over-trading; increasing turnover at the expense of margins.

4   Launching the 'big project' which the company underestimated or could not handle. 'Companies run by autocrats are much more likely than other companies to adopt grandiose schemes'.

5   Over-gearing to the point that even normal business hazards become a constant threat.

6   Deterioration in various financial performance ratios.

7   'Creative accounting' which hid the true situation or hindered prediction. The reader will be able to think of his own examples of companies which have changed their accounting bases more than once, changed their treatment of taxation, or the percentage of profit taken on work in progress, in order to appear to maintain a barely acceptable reported profit level. It cannot go on for ever.

8   'Non-financial' symptoms, such as declines in morale, service, stock availability, or increases in payment periods, complaints. Management begins to get desperate.

9   The last few months, when suppliers demand COD, creditors ask questions, shareholders get restive, the Board gets on its knees to the bank, other 'friendly companies, their wives . . .'.

Every item on these two very similar summaries becomes a Board-level matter when a company is weak. The Director who sees the problems, but does not act remorselessly within the Boardroom to remedy them, can find the subsequent receivership acutely uncomfortable. Firstly, he might get fired by the receiver, who does not have to honour previously existing employment contracts. No golden handshake. Alternatively, he might be kept on a while to do all the dreary things like signing and sealing documents covering decisions taken by others, without his involvement. The receiver does not have to ask his opinion. Being a eunuch is only a mite less humiliating than being treated as a eunuch. Secondly, he might find that the receiver unearths all sorts of strange transactions, about which he had no personal knowledge. The humiliation of emasculation is only a mite less than the humiliation of exposed ignorance. Thirdly, he might just find himself enmeshed in the periphery of, or bang in the middle of, a case for misfeasance, or a claim for damages. In the past, the law allowed only those who had been damaged by an action or inaction to sue, i.e. only the company could sue, and if the company was insolvent, it would not. Today the courts will allow a case to be initiated by a minority shareholder, which will open the way for easier attack on Directors who have proved inadequate.

Certainly there will be more actions against individual Directors in the future. And rightly so. Few would deny that it has long been inequitable that Directors, including both executives and non-executives, could walk away from one disaster into similar roles elsewhere, without public query. The Director owes a duty of 'skill and care' to his company. The Director who sits on his hands when he should, instead, be thumping the Boardroom table with them, is defining his own level of skill and care as being too low to justify his having a seat at that, or any similar, table.

9   *Internal responsibilities*

Electing the Chairman

The CBI recommended in 1973 that Chairmen of public companies should be appointed and re-appointed on a year-by-year basis, since which time the recommendation has received no further comment, perhaps because it smacks of the rankest heresy, or produces visions of corporate anarchy. Yet in view of the near-hypnotic hold which a dominant Chairman can exert over his co-directors, to the detriment of their contribution, and thus to the detriment of the Board's performance, there is huge merit in the CBI's recommendation. Also within private companies.

Because he is the one Director who remains years after the scheduled retiring age; because in current practice he controls entry to the Board; because the media come to identify him as 'the company' and the company as 'him'; because of the very fact that he has been there longer than the rest – the Chairman is usually seen as something akin to the Rock of Gibraltar. His developing eccentricities become very visible alongside the strenuous efforts of his co-directors to avoid all signs of eccentricity. He is called 'Chairman' outside the Board by those who will call even the fiercest Chief Executive 'Adrian' or 'Charles'. And he is the one Director who all the other Directors will agree is pushing through what none of them want, but they let him push it through, anyway. He has become institutionalised. His continuance in office through the thick and the thin, without murmur from the Directors, represents one of the least understood, and least actioned, of all the Board's responsibilities. True, he is often the wisest, or once may have been. But not always, and not forever.

The long dominance of a Board by a powerful Chairman can generate harmful side effects. One-man bands can become bullies. The Chief Executive, and other executive Directors, can lose heart. They will move, if they are good, or sink into submissive obedience if not so good. Ever since Man came down from the trees, stopped chewing greenery and became a hunter, the leader has needed the active cooperation of his group in order to catch their quarry – not passive submission. If the brilliance for which the Chairman was elected in the first place begins to fade, or be overridden by egocentric objectives, the mechanism of Board control will rust and seize fast.

Too often the Chairman is elected to that role after a period as Chief Executive, as though this is a natural progression. It is not. The two roles are fundamentally different, and in most cases require quite different personalities and styles. A newly-elected Chairman who is about to relinquish the Chief Executiveship will seldom promote an equally tough man to succeed him to it. He will seldom lead his Board in critical review of the plans and mechanics which he devised when he was himself Chief Executive. And he will seldom be able to keep his fingers out of the managerial pie, which has to date been his whole life.

One of the non-executives should be better for the Chairmanship, if he has already absorbed himself into the culture of the organisation by chairing a Divisional Board or two. Selecting the right man is not difficult if the non-executives have had close relations with the company, and have been judged in these relationships by the other Directors. Those who only managed to turn up for the monthly meetings disqualify themselves for lack of interest.

The difficulty is not in finding the replacement, whether from within or without. The difficulty is in understanding that the Board really does have both the right and the responsibility to replace an unsuitable Chairman, and then in making its intentions clear to the incumbent. If the Board adopts a 12-monthly re-election routine, this becomes, with a little preliminary lobbying, a great deal easier.

If the charge hand fails to orchestrate his little unit productively, he loses his job. If the sales manager consistently mishandles his sales force, he loses his. If the head of engineering cannot maintain a team which delivers the goods in reliable format, he too is replaced. It should not be different with the Chairman of the Board.

The Chairman manages the Board. The Board, through its Chief Executive, manages the management. The management manages the company's budgeted businesses. If the Chairman manages the Board badly, or not at all, or with objectives which are privately oriented, then the whole chain of innovation, development and control will certainly fail.

Electing the Chief Executive

One-third of our Managing Directors are pretty good; one-third are middling; and one-third are so appallingly bad that I do not know how they survive.

LORD WILFRED BROWN

The Board's most important single decision is the election of a Chief Executive. The vote on this appointment commits the company to a style and standard of operational management which it may live with for many years. It is the most difficult of all decisions to change in the face of later evidence that it was wrong. It is a single vote about a single person, which shackles many Directors with bonds which are real, though wholly unrealistic. Bonds where logic is allowed to be overridden blindly by primaeval loyalty. It can be most difficult, but most necessary, to remember that loyalty must be to the strength and survival of the company, not to a very special kind of colleague. It is the one appointment where the Board should prefer to recruit an outsider if there are any significant doubts about an internal candidate – the exact opposite of normal good practice in preferring existing staff for all other positions.

In the USA around two-thirds of Chief Executive Officers are promoted from within. The pattern of their executive background, prior to moving into general management, differs markedly from the pattern in the UK. More than 2 in 5 come from the marketing function; only 1 in 5 come from the finance function, with a similar proportion from manufacturing/engineering.

In the UK there is an inbuilt assumption that an engineering company can only be headed by an engineer, despite the fact that it can be apparent to the Board that the company's situation requires quite different characteristics. Electing a Chief Executive means matching an individual to a very specific situation. All executive Directors are potential candidates, or should be able to be. All are aware that an incautious word about their future superior can blight their careers. Few therefore contribute actively to this decision, and most judge where to place their vote according to where the centre of gravity seems to lie – which in practice means where the Chairman has made clear he intends to place his vote. Most executives who throw caution to the winds and say precisely what they believe to be true about an inadequate internal candidate, who has the vote of the Chairman (and thus almost certainly has the votes of the one-day-per-month non-executives), do so only in the prior knowledge that they plan to be working elsewhere in the very near future. Yet saying what they believe to be true may indeed be saying the truth, and it is their duty to say it. Executive directorship can demand a distressing level of personal courage.

The Chairman is normally the prime mover in recommending, and where necessary in bludgeoning through, the election of his own preferred candidate to be the Chief Executive who will manage the managers. It can usefully be argued that the Chairman's role is to steer the Board, not the management, and that he should therefore be the least forceful of all in this process. This is true particularly if the Chairman is also the outgoing Chief Executive, and is recommending his own replacement. The probability that he will recommend someone whom he can continue to 'line manage' from the chair, is high. Or, if forced to accept the need to recruit from outside, the chance that he will reject the first round or two of candidates presented is also demonstrably high, on the natural human basis that 'no one can follow me'. But the Chief Executive must not be, nor be open to the charge of being, the 'Chairman's man', his shadow, his younger self, his vicarious power.

Many of the currently prevailing style of one-day-per-month non-executives have the experience, and even the impartiality, to be able to match candidates to the job, but have so little specific knowledge of the people and businesses in the company on whose Board they sit, that they can give little more to this critical decision than the least courageous of the executives. The harmfulness of the casual non-executive is most clearly seen when there is disagreement among the executives about succession. By simple ignorance of their company, or by a lack of practising interest in it, they come to form that very centre of gravity into which the unthinking votes are thrown, thus dispiriting the executives whom they are intended to stimulate.

Where candidature for the position of Chief Executive is not clear cut, or where there is a strong measure of executive disagreement, Boards frequently choose to postpone the final decision by adopting the interim mechanism of appointing two or more joint managing Directors. For any company, other than the very largest, to do this must be wrong. One person must carry the ultimate managerial responsibility; one person must take the most difficult operational decisions. Only one American President can press the button which fires the nuclear missiles. What if there were two? When the joint French and British administrations in the New Hebrides decided to stop playing that charade, out came the bows and arrows.

One bad general does better than two good ones.

NAPOLEON

The placing of multiple Chief Executives on a Holding Board can only make sense if the corporation's businesses really can be divided into a number of divisions which have absolutely no operational overlaps. But then the joint chiefs will need to form a caucus which works out its own preliminary assessments on investment priorities, as best it can, before investment proposals come to the Board for decision. And somebody has to head that caucus and speak for it. A natural leader will almost always emerge.

Worst of all compromises is when a Chairman, who combines the position of Chief Executive, comes close to retirement, but cannot safely slip the Chief Executive role because of the level of Board disagreement about his nominated successor. This is one of the most common reasons for introducing the joint managing Directors mechanism. It is also one of the most dangerous. Directors will find that, come the appointed day for the Chairman to slip his joint managing directorship, they 'really cannot go back on it now', and they will inevitably pass the mantle of Chief Executive to the man about whom so many doubts were expressed not so long before.

If there are any doubts about the qualities or style of an internal candidate for the role of Chief Executive, then he must be rejected. There must be no doubts about the Chief Executive, and least of all in the Boardroom itself. History will certainly place its own verdict on his subsequent performance into the public record.

Appointing other executives

One-third of the short-listed top managers whom I vet are found not suitable for the position concerned; usually because they are not clever enough, or not tough enough to stand up to the pressures.

DOUGLAS MACKENZIE DAVEY,
Industrial Psychologist

Appointments to the Board must be judged on two criteria: whether the candidate's skills will add significantly to the sum of the existing Directors' capabilities, and whether his personality will enable him to contribute actively and consistently to the bulk of the Board's decisions. When recruiting externally, most Boards will carefully judge the candidate against the first criterion, but few will measure him against the second.

Recruitment of senior executives is the most difficult of all management functions. The chances of error are multiplied tenfold when the appointment also involves a seat in the Boardroom. There are personality-analysing techniques which can be employed, ranging from interview by psychologists, to gobbledegook question-and-answer papers which produce miraculously accurate descriptions, to handwriting analysis, or graphology, now almost a science, certainly a 'fine art', and very far from its black-magic image in the UK. The Germans frequently use it when making senior appointments; the French always use it. The writer has used it with quite dramatically accurate results. Such techniques are never 100 per cent foolproof, but added to the judgement of the recruiting panel they can powerfully reinforce subjective conclusions, or open new lines of enquiry, which may unearth characteristics which would be harmful in the position concerned. Yet few UK companies insist that such techniques be used. Most recruitment consultants eschew them. And some candidates refuse to be tested by them – often with good reason.

It is surprising that prevailing practice for recruiting senior executives in the UK boils down to the Board selecting someone from a handful of possibles presented to it by an executive search consultant, or 'head hunter'. Surprising, because one would not expect the Board to be satisfied by applying its judgement to such a small catchment only, which has been compiled at the judgement of an organisation which does not carry the Board's responsibilities. Certainly the process of recruiting senior people is so often fraught with internal politics, power chasing, and plain ignorance of what the Board really needs, that each senior appointment should only be made with the help of a truly professional recruitment consultant, who provides both an unprejudiced evaluation of the type of person needed and an unprejudiced evaluation of the candidates located.

Some of the head hunters are truly professional. Few are psychologists; almost as few have worked in senior management; very few have sweated in the Boardroom hot-house in the kind of industrial and commercial companies which they serve. Most can offer little more than conclusions and recommendations based on the apparent message from references, notoriously unreliable, and the apparent nature of a career history and 'track record'.

Time and again someone who has made an appalling blunder in one company is head-hunted smartly out to an equivalent role in another company, carrying no doubt the glad references of colleagues who are only too happy to see him go. Only space and the laws of libel prevent this from being illustrated, but the reader will know his own examples.

Too often the references and the record are deceptive. Too often the head hunter, without the aid of the personality-analysing techniques which he does not routinely use, is no more able to spot an alcoholic or a schizophrenic than any other layman. And these categories do get appointed to Boards. If the writer has seen examples, so has the reader.

Seldom do head hunters relate their own conclusions about a candidate to a judgement on how he will be able to interrelate with his proposed new co-directors; often as not they only meet one or two of those Directors. Seldom do they analyse the business situation into which the successful candidate will be slotted; few are equipped by managerial experience to do so. The use of head hunters for the recruitment of senior executives in the UK is today almost universal, and really senior posts are almost never advertised in the press as they were, as a routine, only a decade ago. The performance of British Boards has not improved during the decade. The mushroom growth of this recruiting technique may, perhaps, not be blamed for that – but it has not effected any improvements either.

The recruitment of senior staff is such an important Board responsibility that the Directors most closely concerned could benefit by stepping back a pace, pausing, and giving a little logical consideration to how they go about it. The process of head hunting grew up in the USA where there was no nationally distributed newspaper which would be read regularly by the nationwide catchment of potential top-level executives. Recruitment advertising could therefore be rather hit-and-miss, and a 'search' for likely candidates could make sense. (But so could geographically localised advertising; the executive dug into sunny California might be reluctant to move to New Jersey. It is a big country, and Americans are becoming less mobile, not more so. Many of the US 'searches' are geographically confined.)

The same conditions do not apply within the UK and Europe. In a few European countries head hunting is against the law, although it does continue. For some reason, a number of Directors seem to be stimulated by working in this manner, even if it means being party to a breach of those laws. In some European countries all vacant positions have to be advertised by law, either in the company's name or through a professional, such as a lawyer, accountant, or consultant.

The primary arguments used in favour of head hunting are that: top executives do not read the jobs ads; and the best people working successfully, do not want to move, and have to be drawn out to better things (i.e. better for them) by covert, rather than overt, means.

The largest recruitment consultancy in the world, which carries out both head hunting and recruitment advertising, has gone into print that the first argument, in their unrivalled experience, is simply 'not true'. Witness also the extent to which the head hunters themselves use advertising, for example when recruiting head hunters. Or the way in which they obtain coverage in the 'Jobs Column' of the *Financial Times*, which is quite simply free advertising.

The second argument must raise a chuckle. If a man really does not want to move, he will not. Or should not. The implication that someone else knows what is better for his career than he does himself only raises doubts about his own judgement. The pity is that the 'under the wraps' approach seems to be just as titillating to some men as it is to the Chairmen who sanction it.

The search process is far from mysterious. It is simple. That is why so many ill-equipped organisations have set up as head hunters, to the detriment of that much smaller number of really experienced and professional executive search firms which can, and do, actually help companies. Truth also is that the recruitment consultant makes a bigger fee, on average with much less work, by head hunting than by taking a percentage on advertisements. Their words, not the writer's.

If companies took the trouble to try recruiting by advertising and by head hunting simultaneously, they would get some surprises. Time and again old-fashioned advertising has been demonstrated to bring in more suitable staff. Maybe not always, but certainly often enough to suggest that the Board which does not advertise has absolutely no reason for confidence, ever, that recruiting without advertising has located the best men it could appoint to conduct the affairs of its company. The Board is responsible for the quality of the men who conduct the affairs of its company. There is something faintly ridiculous about a Board delegating the largest part of its single largest responsibility to outsiders. Something more than ridiculous about a Board working on the assumption that these outsiders – any outsiders, however competent – can really locate all the relevant good men without advertising. The writer has seen it demonstrated, often, that they cannot.

Besides critically reducing the area covered, recruiting without advertising also denies the Board the opportunity to meet a variety of candidates who might fill other slots, actual or potential. And it removes, or severely reduces, the opportunity to obtain some insights into the competitors by meeting applicants from such companies – one of the more useful by-products of the advertising and interview process.

For effective and responsible recruiting:

1 Establish a committee of the Board, comprising the Chairman, the Chief Executive, one other executive Director and a non-executive. Charge the committee with vetting the draft job specification drawn up by the Chief Executive, and perhaps helping to improve it.

2 Select an experienced recruitment consultant. If necessary talk to several and vet them as rigorously as you will vet the candidates. Involve the selected consultant from the outset, including in finalising the job specification. Let him know whatever he wants to know about the job, the company, the Board. The better he is, the more he is likely to ask.

3 Advertise widely, either in the company's name, or in the name of a professional firm, dependent on the circumstances of the vacancy.

4 Perhaps also head hunt if the job specification is unusual, or if a very specific industry background really is required, for example when recruiting a Technical Director. Vet the head hunter, too, as rigorously as you will vet the candidates.

5 Ensure that all the replies are seen by the committee and consultant. The time wasters and the unqualified may number 180 out of 200, but they are quickly put aside.

6   Compile a long list of possibles and probables. Reduce to about a dozen by discussion between the committee and the consultant.

   Do not reject men who are older than the age considered ideal. (They are probably not as old as your Chairman.) Age discrimination is already illegal in the US, Canada, France and elsewhere, and such legislation must become more widespread.

   Do not reject men who are redundant, self-employed or unemployed just because they are one of these things. If they look interesting on paper, but you are worried why they are not in employment, ask them why they are not. They may have a better reason for having left their last job than many a senior executive has for staying in his. The Americans do not discriminate against the man who is not in employment, but this foolish practice is prevalent in the UK. Someone who is 'up against it' because of age or unemployment will prove less likely to flit about and treat your company like a stepping-stone (Now that rang a bell, didn't it?).

7   Interview the dozen or so, with committee and consultant all present.

8   If the head hunt has produced a couple of heads, include them and treat them just the same as the others. They are no different, whatever the head hunter may say, or they would not be talking to you. If a head-hunted candidate emphasises how difficult it will be to winkle him out of the marvellous job he is doing elsewhere, drop him. If he does not want you as much as you want a good man, he is not your man. If he has to be seduced by paying him more than other good men, he is not worth the extra. The concept that the only person worth having is someone who really does not want to move is a myth. It is also a nonsense; that must be self evident. Yet this is a standard part of the patter of a number of the recruitment consultants who specialise only in head hunting. If the man has not the sensitivity to rapidly determine that the job may 'fit', or if he has strong initial doubts, it will not.

9 Whittle down to three or four. Put these through
professional psychological testing. If any object, let
them drop out. People should want to know their
true personality characteristics; this is part of
honing their own effectiveness. Remember that
straight head hunting, or recruitment without
personality testing, will at best tell you 'what a
person has done', not always whether he has really
done it well, and never, repeat never, what he really
can do and achieve. Every job is different; what he
has done in one may bear little relation to what he
can do in another job, or another environment.
Further, the record of 'what he has done' is often
nebulous, or is just a record of what others have
done for him, or is intentionally misleading.

10 Whittle down to two or three; and present these to
the full Board. The Board has time; it is not going to
be doing anything more important on that day. And
it takes a lot more time to clear up the shambles
after the subsequent removal of an unsuitable
recruit.

11 Collectively agree on the best candidate. Ask the
remuneration committee to settle his pay and perquisites package; they can do it straight away as
they are sitting at the same table and can go next
door for five minutes.

12 Tell the selected candidate. Take up references if
you have to, for example if technical competence
needs a level of confirmation which could not be
achieved in interview. Remember that no one will
give bad references, even if deserved, and few will
give accurate references, so you are left to rely on the
Board's subjective judgement, plus the psychologist's objective judgement. The psychologist,
and very often the skilled graphologist, should at
least be able to determine if the man concerned is a
conman or a liar. The writer has seen both
categories exposed by such analyses, and later confirmed by hard facts.

13 Call him in to fix final details, including his initial
induction. In his first two or three weeks he can ask

all the silly questions he likes without damaging his standing. During that period his colleagues will enjoy supplying him with any relevant information. After that he is on his own.

If on the other hand the Board has decided to promote an internal candidate, it should still use the opportunity to induce the person concerned to be put through the same aptitude and personality tests as would be used for an external candidate for the Board. A manager should welcome (fear a little, but welcome) being put through them at this most critical point in his whole career path. Some multinationals, such as ITT, always put internally-promoted executives through psychological analysis before their promotion is confirmed.

Character, mental condition, and thus aptitude to handle a Board position, often change measurably around the same time as a person reaches Board level, because most of the stresses and changes in his life, including domestically, occur at around this time. The Board has to determine whether the candidate can handle the change from being a manager only, to being a manager part of the time and a Director the other part; whether he can handle a situation at the Board where he has to disagree with his superior, the Chief Executive, and press an opposing case. A good Chief Executive is aware that he is no graven image, and he grows and flourishes under stimulus. The key to balancing the Board is to ensure that the mix of Directors does provide a constant stimulus to both thinking and performance. Executives appointed to the Board need to be measured against this requirement.

When a Director fails, because he has slowly declined in one way or another, or because his job has evolved beyond his capabilities, or because he was badly recruited in the first place, the Board has to stiffen its resolve and remove him, sideways or out. The problem in carrying inert ballast or dangerous cargo is not that it costs a few thousands to have it on Board. It costs that much to decorate the romp room each year. The problem is that the non-contributor deadens. He pulls down the level of your game. He fills a seat which someone else could use more profitably.

The real trouble lies in the self-perpetuation of the mediocre; of managers who are never brilliant and never atrocious, but whose use of the assets is less effective than the dumbest shareholder could manage for himself.

ROBERT HELLER,
The Naked Manager

The removal of inadequate Directors is today most commonly accompanied by the payment of a large golden handshake, often beyond contract limits. This gives huge offence to the remaining executives, or to those who read about it in the press. And it is often no more than a buying-out by the Board for having abrogated its prime responsibility of recruiting intelligently in the first place.

Appointing non-executives

Prevailing practice is that the Chairman decides when the Board needs a non-executive; talks with his business contacts for suggested names to supplement his own catchment; selects the man he judges suitable; presents him to the full Board, or to a committee of the Board, for approval on the nod.

Because most other Directors are passive throughout this process, it cannot be surprising that the average non-executive is viewed as 'the Chairman's man' from the first day he walks into the Boardroom, whether or not he was originally selected to be just that. He becomes identified with his sponsor, and he remains in unison with him through the thick and the thin. His value to the Board is small, or negative.

The tacit assumption is that the Chairman, as the leader of the Board, carries the sole responsibility for ensuring that the composition of the Board is soundly balanced. Naturally this is a responsibility of the Chairman, but it is not his alone. Indeed, where the Chairman is by character autocratic, it will inevitably be the other Directors who sense most keenly the need to introduce an element of counter balance.

Any single Director who believes that his Boardroom needs a little more independent objectivity, or any other category of part-time participation, should marshal his facts, lobby his co-directors mercilessly, and insist that the matter be itemised on the next agenda. If voted down, but still aware that the need remains, he should return to the fray after the passage of a few more months have helped to demonstrate, more strongly, the case which he is seeking to make. It is a nerve-wracking exercise, which few Directors will care to undertake more than once. It can be made a great deal less awkward if the Board has an annual spot on the agenda to review Board composition, to review the performance and contribution of the existing non-executives, and thus to collectively decide, as a routine, whether changes need to be made.

The appointment of a new non-executive should be as methodically conducted as the appointment of a new executive. The Board should:

1 Establish a committee of the Board, consisting of the Chairman, two other non-executives, if there are any, and one executive. The total should be three or four. Whether or not to include the Chief Executive is a moot point; should he be a primary judge of someone whose primary role will be to judge him in the future? When a subsidiary Board is looking for a non-executive, the Chief Executive is best included in the committee; the deliberations of a down line Board will always be much closer to management matters.

2 Provide the committee with a broad statement of the observed needs of the Board in terms of background and style of candidate required, seen against the main strategic problems and opportunities facing the company, and against the existing backgrounds and styles already represented on the Board.

3 Require the committee to refine these terms of reference to a format which can be advertised, while still keeping the catchment area broad. The Board will always be looking for widely-based business experience and an unprejudiced, lively judgement, not for specialists in ultra-violet radiation technology, nor the manufacture of thermoplastics,

nor the distribution of silk neckties. If it does not already employ people with sufficient expertise in its mainstream businesses, it should engage some, or hire a technical consultant.

> *The value of the directors to the shareholders lies not so much in their technical or professional qualifications as in their personal qualities, amongst them the wise and practical judgement they can bring to the attitudes of the company.*

CBI, 1973

4   Empower the committee to select a recruitment consultant well experienced in the field of non-executives. Be prepared to pay him a fee which reflects the amount of work which he will be expected to do. For some reason, many companies do not want to pay as much for assistance in recruiting a non-executive as they pay for assistance in recruiting a junior manager. Use the independent judgement of the consultant to check that the brief produced by the committee does match observed needs. The consultant, if he is any good, will want to meet and speak with most of the Directors, to determine their personalities and styles.

5   Empower the committee to advertise, whether in the company's name or in the name of a professional firm. There is a wider range of first-rate talent available than is known to any of the best recruitment consultants. Advertising will produce a much wider spread of alternatives than will result from a simple head hunt, or from a file search in the offices of the consultant.

6   Leave the committee and the consultant to trim the alternatives to 2 or 3, who are then presented to the full Board.

7   Concentrate on the candidates with the most varied background and most flexible approach. If the Board is looking for just one non-executive, and particularly if he is the first non-executive to be

appointed to that Board, do not go for the narrower background, even if it seems more directly relevant to the most burning problems of the moment; this may delimit too tightly the Board's subsequent vision of what the non-executive contribution, in general, can produce over the years.

8   Double-check in full Board that the selected candidate really does meet the original specification within reasonable limits, and that both he and all the Board members fully understand what, and how much, he is intended to contribute, including in terms of time and geography. If he will be unable to visit the units in Aberdeen or Abu Dhabi, then he probably is not going to be able to do much else either. Anything less than an average of two days per month is not worth the trouble or expense of appointing him, in all but the very fewest cases. Smaller companies, or subsidiaries, may realistically require more than that. If it needs three or four days per month for a year or so, then the time to ensure that he can, and will, give this commitment is before he is appointed.

9   Post-decision, establish an initial programme of induction, so that the new non-executive can be a useful contributor within weeks, not months. Agree his routine information requirements, and how they will be met. Establish dates for future meetings, including Boards, committees, planning sessions. Introduce him briefly, but rapidly, to all senior managers. Give him:

> current management and financial accounts;
> brief company history and recent past accounts;
> budgets, plans, investment appraisals, special study reports;
> structure diagrams, with names of senior men and brief details of their remuneration and other conditions, and their backgrounds;
> detailed trade literature;
> copies of the last year's minutes.

10   Annually review his, and every other Director's,

performance, if necessary amending the agreed roles of the non-executive, or changing him.

The annual performance review should be as cold-blooded as the initial selection process. The person appointed may have lost interest halfway through the year, and this will have shown. Or he may have found that, with the best will in the world, he cannot provide the time which the company needs.

For good reasons or bad, the majority of existing non-executives do not or cannot meet the terms of reference against which they were appointed – if indeed such terms were ever agreed at all. Most Boards still monitor the performance of their non-executives less rigorously than they monitor a junior clerk.

People and organisation

The Board's management-related responsibilities concern people, planning and performance. The three are inter-meshed; there can be no effective management of performance without adequate consideration of the placing and relationships of key people, and there can be no realistic planning without a close knowledge of both the aspirations and limitations of those people.

Chapter 3 considered the Board's responsibility for establishing, and maintaining in good working order, a companywide mechanism for participation and communication. Communication is more than informing; it requires the two-way interchange of understanding. If employees do not understand what the Board is doing, and why, or vice versa, then the mechanism needs an overhaul.

The mechanism for participation and communication must parallel the company's control structure, through all the layers of the company. If it does not do so, confusion will arise naturally, or will be made to arise by those who feed on confusion – either on the staff, or outside it. The Board's control structure must enable policy decisions, and subsequent management decisions, to pass as rapidly and smoothly downwards and outwards as any simple piece of information which requires no action. Divisionalisation, centralisation, the size and grouping of subsidiaries, the composition of divisional and subsidiary Boards, the parallel creation of operating committees and the cross-boundary liaison machinery between units of the company are all matters for which the Board is responsible.

The control structure must 'work'. The Board is responsible for ensuring that it does so, and for changing it when it does not. It can only determine that it does not if data for the Boardroom from any area is disorganised, if decisions from the Boardroom are not acted on in the manner, or to the timetable, described, or if staff to whom the Directors speak outside of the Boardroom express concern. The quickest and surest criterion is the last of these three. If more Directors spent more time talking to more managers outside of the Boardroom, then more companies would operate more efficiently, more quickly.

The performance of the Board will always depend on how effectively the structure can carry out the decisions taken in the Boardroom. The best structure is always first defined in theory, and then adapted in practice to fit the characteristics of the key people who will carry out those decisions. Whichever aspect of Board responsibility we look at, we return to the fundamental responsibility of knowing and understanding the key people, outside the Boardroom, on whom corporate performance will always depend.

Sometimes the structure itself can inhibit the best of people. There is one large UK Group which has long operated a corporate 'matrix' structure of vertical design-and-production units, and a superimposed horizontal series of international marketing units. At each intersection between the vertical and horizontal sits a territorial market, with a described range of products to be promoted for sale within it. The head of the horizontal marketing line believes he is responsible for all local decisions, be they pricing, licensing, distribution or whatever. The head of the vertical line believes precisely the same. Sometimes success is achieved at one 'intersection' by the tougher minded of the two simply refusing to cooperate with anyone else, excluding anyone else from knowledge of what he intends to do in that market, and doing it. He succeeds by breaking all the corporate rules. The markets are as bewildered by all this as the managers, but they cannot do anything about it. The Board can. It does not. The company does not do very well overseas.

The Chief Executive is naturally the prime mover in evaluating and proposing an optimum organisational structure for the company. His opinion weighs heavier than that of the other Directors, not only because he should be the best informed, but because he is charged with operational responsibility, and must be given his head as far as the Board judges possible. But the Board must consciously judge.

The Chief Executive might, for example, prefer to differentiate and separate the subsidiaries when some of his co-directors might conclude that the merging of several of them would be more effective. He might choose to divide and rule because that makes his life simpler – a valid enough reason if it does not reduce corporate potential. He might be wrong for good or bad reasons. He will always judge from a personal viewpoint; the Board must always judge from a corporate viewpoint. The viewpoints may, or may not, coincide.

A new Chief Executive from outside the company will, almost invariably, seek to introduce organisational structures close to his immediate past experience. All organisms seek the minimum of simultaneous change, and the new Chief Executive may want to carry his environment with him, like the hermit crab which always chooses the empty shells of exactly the same species of snail as it grows from one size to a larger.

It might just be that the Chief Executive will perform best in an operational environment defined by himself to meet his own operating characteristics. But it might also be that the unique entity which is 'the company' will itself thrive best under wholly different constraints. The objective of Board responsibility, indeed the objective in having a Board at all, is to ensure that the company is guided by professional rather than by personal conclusions.

Like any organic entity, the company is constantly changing, and often very rapidly. Different types of organisation, and different relationships between men, are required at different stages in growth. Companies most frequently hit problems when moving through a 'growth step'. The problems are commonly exaggerated because the Board does not recognise that the company has reached such a 'step'. Or because, when it does recognise that the company is changing, it does not ensure that the organisational structure and interrelationships are methodically realigned from top to bottom to take account of the changes. The Board nearly always acts too slowly, leaving such moves to its down-line managers, who will not 'get it right' because they see only a part of the whole picture.

The Board can avoid being caught out by change if it gives an annual, or half-yearly spot on the agenda to organisation and structure. This would slot neatly into the annual, or half-yearly, budgeting and planning programme, being also part and parcel of any responsible review of the company's future.

Planning

A man who does not think and plan long ahead will find trouble right by his door.

CONFUCIUS

In the 1960s the buzz-word was 'marketing'. In the early 1970s it was replaced at the top of the list of Board enthusiasms by 'business planning', or 'strategic' or 'corporate' planning, which are fundamentally the same, though some specialists insist on defining nuances of difference between them.

The real-life interface between marketing and planning became blurred. The essentially simple planning process developed a religion and jargon of its own. It became so complex and theory-ridden that many companies, especially the smaller ones which had most need of it, almost welcomed the dislocations of 1973/4 as demonstrating that the world in general, and their companies in particular, were quite clearly unplannable. Companies, large and small, trimmed back their planning department, where they had one, at just the time they had greatest need for it.

Any company which is working today without formalised

planning routines is assuredly placing its survival at risk. Any company which is not budgeting and monitoring within a planned longer-term strategy is rudderless in a sea which will never be calm. The planning process is indeed essentially simple, but it involves a lot of work; it involves digging-up previously unquestioned assumptions, and examining the corporate whole from its roots to its greenest shoots.

It begins with the Board defining and communicating a set of policies against which the company and its individual units can compile and evaluate their plans. Strikingly few Boards have ever drawn up such a statement of policies, let alone amended them and communicated the amendments when the business environment changed, thereby demonstrating to their companies that they were alive to their situation.

The Board's first attempt at defining its policies can be simple. It can refine them with time. No one down line will quibble about one or two points being left out, or being inadequately covered; they will welcome any guidance they can get as to how the Board is thinking. The policies should include:

- its fundamental beliefs, if it truly has some. For example, the importance of individual contribution and reward, and of whole-hearted autonomy. Or alternatively, the belief that coordinated biggest is best, with strongly centralised control leading to collective performance and collective gain; or whatever else identifies a corporate ethic, if there is one;
- what the company aims to achieve, in which businesses, where, how much – what the company is not, and will not do;
- its policy for business development, whether at home or overseas, by acquisition, diversification, organic growth;
- its criteria for such growth, and how proposals for investment and development will be handled;
- its criteria for the returns required for survival and growth; an ROC at X per cent above the rate of borrowing; a profit progression at Y per cent above the rate of inflation;
- its policy for the control and charging out of the cost of its 'centre', including interest (so that unit pricing can be

realistic, and so that the centre itself can be seen to be exposed);

- its policy for employee remuneration – for example, middle of the top or middle quartile for the industry – and its routines for appraisal, induction, training, promotion and recruitment of employees; incentive schemes, if any;
- its management structure, with its advisory or executive committees and their functions and limitations; its parallel structure for participation and communication, the routing of suggestions and complaints, and how these will be handled;
- external relations, and how they will be handled, including customers, suppliers, government departments, trade associations, the media, as well as the competition;
- the planning and budgeting routines which flow from the above, and the monitoring and control machinery.

The Board is responsible for compiling such policies, for defining the objectives which derive directly from them, and for describing the basic strategies by which the objectives will be achieved.

The policies are 'statements of intent', which provide guidelines for management. The objectives are 'desired performance results', which describe what the Board wants the company to achieve, when. Most are quantified, and against a timescale:

- a reduction in working capital by X per cent in Y years;
- an increase in ROC by W per cent in Z years;
- an increase in direct exports from M per cent to N per cent of turnover in P years;
- a reduction in staff turnover from R to S per cent per annum in T years – and so on through all the areas of Board responsibility.

The strategies are the 'how'. While policies and objectives are exclusively Board matters, the strategies are part-Board, part-management responsibilities. They run through the whole of the plan period, which may be 3, 5 or 20 years, depending on the level of Board concerned, or the size of company.

The tactics are the 'immediate how', and are reflected in the detailed expenditures reçorded in the one-year budget. They should always fall within the wider strategies, and represent step one in applying those strategies as the plan period opens.

When introducing formalised planning, the Board will need to use a common approach for all units, including a common set of forms to be filled, otherwise it will not be able to make rapid and meaningful comparisons between units, nor coherently compose a corporate picture. It will find that managers who are not already used to these disciplines will view any such forms as 'more nonsense from head office', so the first round formats must be kept quite basic. They should ask only those questions which any manager, given a push, can agree he should be asking himself, which are directly related to the analysis of his business, and the answers to which will help him produce better results in the future. They must include:

1   A covering description on the way the formats are to be completed, with worked examples, if there can be any doubts. A statement of the number of years to be covered (three is quite enough at the first attempt) and the rate of inflation and bank interest to be used for each year. Both of these may turn out to be wrong, but the Board will need data which has been compiled against the same yardsticks by all units.

2   A review of the main external factors which the unit believes will affect performance during the plan period, either positively or negatively, including critical factors which could kill or maim it.

3   An analysis of existing and planned markets and businesses, which breaks the total business of the unit into a number of definably different activities. One of the objectives of the planning process is to isolate those activities which should be de-emphasised or closed, and those on which the unit should concentrate its time and resources. Each company, however small, has at least half-a-dozen definably

different activities, whether defined by different types of customer, different ranges of products, different competitors, different methods of selling, or any one of a series of similar criteria.

4 A quantitative analysis of the performance, by sales, gross margin and net profit, of each of these definably different activities in the past year, the current year, and as anticipated in each year of the plan period. Every unit, be sure, will say that such analysis is quite impossible, because of shared overheads, overlapping markets, or absence of base data. They always do. Every unit, be equally sure, can be made to complete suitable analyses, and every unit will get a surprise from completing them. The exercise always highlights that the unit is bleeding from one activity, or from several, which should have been staunched or amputated long since. Few Directors will readily admit that a business activity which they personally conceived and nurtured some years ago has become a helpless cripple, and by now cries out for mercy-killing. Every company, large or small, subsidiary or independent, continues to nursemaid for years a number of haemophilic activities. Where the bleeders are recognised by the Board, and it determines that it cannot itself bring them back to health, there are no responsible alternatives but to close, or sell to someone with a different kind of marketing medicine. But the bleeders are not always known to the Board. In every company which the writer has looked at, from the inside or from the outside, it has been possible to uncover, by analysis of this kind, one or more activities which were draining resources. There is no company which could not improve performance by such analysis, either by the Board, or with a little external support. The simplest way to improve performance and generate more cash is to stop losing it. If the whole planning process ceased at this point, it would have achieved much.

5 An analysis of the main competitors in each of the defined activities, quantified as best possible by

market shares. Record how the unit sees its own, and their, shares changing during the plan period.

6 A review of moves expected from the competition during the plan period, whether marketing moves, organisational moves (a merging of competitors, or their geographical extension) or the introduction of new products or services – and how the unit plans to respond. The primary element in a company's environment is its competition. Success is measured by how well you do in comparison with your competition. A major element of the company's planning is how it will meet and overcome such competition.

7 A cold-blooded review of the company's strengths and weaknesses, including external competitive and internal performance weaknesses; the moves it plans to make to capitalise on its strengths, and to eliminate its weaknesses, of both kinds. Unless required, formally, to think out and spell out these moves, it may do nothing at all, or do much less than the Board judges necessary.

8 A quantified statement of the resources required to achieve its plan, including money and men. This may, for example, trigger a training programme.

9 A draft budget for each year of the plan, plus a forecast balance sheet for each year end, and cash generated or consumed. The formats may have to be tailored a little for different units at this point, but not so much that the Board cannot readily sum the requirements, sum the returns, and compile a first view of the best and worst corporate situation through the plan period.

All the unit plans come back to the board, via the planning committee, for manipulation, and final approval. The first year of the plan becomes the one-year budget, to which the units are required to operate, and against which their success is monitored. The process is a rolling cycle of policies, objectives, strategies, plans, operations, monitoring – and consequent amending of any of the policies, objectives, strategies, plans or operations which are found to be imperfect.

The Board initiates the cycle, and powers its continuous momentum. The value of the process depends as much on the quality of the monitoring as on the reality of the original policies and objectives; these can always be amended in the light of experience. Both the production of the plans and the monitoring of their suitability demand a great deal of the Directors' time, both within and outside the Boardroom. Which is one reason for the recommendation in Chapter 10 that the process be coordinated by a Board committee. But if reaching a final judgement on any one year's plans, and on the one-year budget which flows from them, means that the whole Board has to lock itself away for a few days in a quiet country house, so be it. The Board has no greater managerial responsibility.

Performance

The processes of recruiting, structuring, policy making and planning are but preambles to the gritty business of generating sufficient returns to be able to survive and grow. The critical point in the closed loop of Board control is receiving the 'feed-back' and applying corrective action; is monitoring the performance or managing the managements.

The smaller the company, the more detailed the content of the feed-back signal. For even the largest, the minimum content needed monthly for making corrective judgements includes:

- a monthly comparison against budgets of orders, sales, costs, overheads, gross and net margins, cash generated or consumed;
- a cumulative year-to-date comparison against budgets of the same elements, plus-or-minus comparison against the past, perhaps on a moving annual total basis; order data should always include the gross margins calculated and the net margins anticipated; gross margin trends, past year/year-to-date/current month/order book, can be one of the best indications of impending trouble.

These comparisons should be accompanied by verbal

explanation of reasons, and recommended corrective actions, at the Board, by the Chief Executive;
- a Chief Executive's running forecast of year-end results; his monthly report will pick up some of the main features or problems, but not all the individual details, on which he can comment verbally;
- a month-end balance, and an updated cash flow forecast; verbal explanations, and recommendations, at the Board by the Finance Director;
- a listing of phased, overdue debtors above a figure determined by the Board, with comparisons against last month's situation which can evidence progress made; and commentary by the Finance Director;
- similarly for creditors; the objective is to keep the trends in debtors and creditors constantly before the Board.
    .Plus, at choice:
- selected ratios, chosen in accordance with the characteristics of the individual trading units – for example, turnover-to-working capital trends; net margins-to-working capital; tenders submitted-to-tenders won, also showing trends. Ratios, and trends in ratios, can frequently highlight actions to be taken more sharply than absolute data can achieve. The good general manager will spot the trends, and tell the Chief Executive what he intends to do about them, before the Chief Executive begins to draft his report.
    Plus:
- external comparisons against moves by the competition during the month, and how the company has reacted; verbal commentary by the Business Development Director. Success is always comparative; the marketplace makes it so. In the late 1970s, for example, an electronics components distributor or insurance broker might have been well pleased with an ROC of 25 per cent. But the industry norms for both categories in that period were almost twice as high. A carpet manufacturer or shipowner might have been desolate with an ROC of 10 per cent. But their industries managed only between 9 and 3 per cent (*ICC Business Ratios*, 1980).

The Chief Executive should ensure that someone in the company is keeping a close watch on comparative industry performance data, ideally a member of the planning office. If the Chief Executive, and his units, are well informed on their comparative internal and external situations, and if the monitoring machinery is working like clockwork, then the managements, through the Chief Executive, should be presenting each monthly Board with predetermined conclusions regarding remedial actions – not simply presenting a bundle of facts, and waiting for the Board to decide what to do about them.

When the Board maintains the machinery in good working order, the Board 'monitors'. When it does not, it has to 'manage'.

10 Mechanics of the Boardroom

The Board's responsibilities are faced and discharged within the Boardroom, at meetings of the Directors operating collectively, making collective decisions, and carrying collective responsibility. Defined parts of these responsibilities may be delegated, if the articles so permit, to committees, or to individuals such as the managing Director, operating effectively as a Board 'committee of one'. But actions and decisions of committees or individuals must be confirmed in the Boardroom; delegation does not mean abrogation.

Meetings

Meetings of Directors are the machinery of the Board, indeed are the sole machinery for exercising Board responsibility and control. The mechanics of the meetings must be smooth; the meetings themselves need not be. The Board should:

- determine how many days after the end of a month are needed to compile the figures for that month (let us say seven days);
- agree that all Board papers, including management and financial accounts for the month past, are posted to all Directors within two days of the date on which the figures are available (therefore post on the ninth);
- allow three to five days from receipt of papers to date of Board meeting (assuming receipt on the tenth day of the month, meetings can be on the thirteenth to the fifteenth). Establish a forward programme of Board meetings six to twelve months ahead, and keep it updated. If possible choose 'the third Monday in the

month', or a similar routine which makes planning ahead more simple, especially for the non-executives;

- meet once a month. Not less. Skip holiday August if you must, but ensure that an ad hoc committee of the Board looks at the figures in that month also, and takes appropriate actions. (In times of crisis, meet fortnightly or weekly. Charge the executive committee with meeting weekly, even daily, until the pressure eases. Circulate the minutes of Boards and committees to all Directors without delay – those who were unable to attend can telephone comments. In times of crisis, all corners of the company turn to the Board, relying on the speed of its action and reaction. Even those corners which have studiously avoided talking to it in the past. In times of crisis, the true commitment, and true availability, of the non-executives is exposed, to their credit or discredit);

- charge the Company Secretary with ensuring that papers, agenda, minutes, management and financial accounts are all collated and despatched by the ninth day of the month (if that is the date which has been calculated). The Secretary's line boss is normally the Chief Executive, but the Chairman or his office should check each ninth that the deadline has been met. It is the Chairman's meeting which will be a mess if there are any hitches;

- ensure that a quorum is always present, even at ad hoc meetings. The 'Table A quorum' is two, but many companies' Articles have increased this to three. Check your Articles, you may get a surprise. An ad hoc meeting can be called at a few moments' notice, assuming that all the Directors to be involved agree to it. Minutes of such a meeting must be tabled at the next full Board, but it is wise to circulate them immediately, so that all the Directors know what is happening. In theory a meeting short of a quorum can also take decisions (for example, an ad hoc meeting of two Directors, when the quorum is three), but these decisions only become valid if subsequently ratified by every single member of the Board. This theoretical mechanism is fraught with risk, and should never be applied. The writer has seen a company bankrupt itself by commitments entered into by such an ad hoc meeting which did not contain a quorum, which did not inform the other Directors quickly enough for the others to countermand the destructive decisions made, and which did not obtain the subsequent ratification of all the Directors;

— remember always that voting in the Boardroom is by simple majority of the Directors, not by shareholding. The Chairman may own 55 per cent of the shares, but he does not thereby have authority to determine what the Board will decide. He has one vote, plus a casting vote in the event of a tie (if the Articles so permit). Very occasionally a company's Articles give special, additional, voting rights to one or more Directors, or to categories of Director. If this is the case in your company, try to obtain the Board's agreement to ask the next General Meeting to alter that Article. If all Directors are not truly equal, and are not treated as equal at the Board table, then the Boardroom process becomes a charade;

— remember that the Board should not need to vote frequently. Directors should normally find that a common agreement can be reached on most points. The Chairman's role is to steer the Board to such agreement when he judges it truly represents responsible unanimity, not weak compromise. Occasionally the Board will remain split. The Chairman must then judge whether to take a vote and reach a majority decision, or to postpone decision until further information has been produced and the Directors have had more chance to weigh the pros and cons. If the matter is not urgent, delay is the best policy. Voting down a minority can be distressing for the minority; it can also mean taking the wrong decision;

> *Decision by majorities is as much an expedient as lighting by gas.*
>
> GLADSTONE

— keep the meetings brisk, but not brusque. While this is primarily the Chairman's responsibility, the other Directors can greatly help. They can sense when the Chairman is seeking to curtail a discussion which deserves more time, and can usually judge the rightness or wrongness of his reasons for doing so. The effective Chairman will ensure that all viewpoints are fully and responsibly expressed. He does have the final authority to decide when 'enough' has been said, and it can be difficult for him to let someone press on with a line of argument with which he strongly disagrees. But this is what differentiates a good Chairman from a bad one, not how quickly he brings you to AOB. If a once-monthly Board meeting lasts less than about two hours, are the Directors really in touch? And in control?

— remember that, while a Director with a burning passion or a deep-felt concern may 'have said it all a dozen times' to his co-directors outside the Boardroom, the only place where he can obtain a Board hearing and a Board decision on his subject of concern is within the Boardroom at a formal Board meeting. He has to put his case there. If he does not, he cannot grumble that the Chairman is a bully. That is why he is a Director, not just a manager;

— ensure that the dissentient is given free air. If his case is irrelevant, it will show. If it is not, he will help the company.

The style of the Boardroom meeting must be open, equal, impartial, patient. Occasionally also unpredictable, surprising, outrageous. Even the ridiculous has its place. A large loss-making company was once in trouble because, while it was winning a few tenders, it was losing most by being 10 to 20 per cent more expensive than its competition. One Director suggested it should increase all its prices. Ridiculous, apparently, but he had guessed that the company was also winning tenders by margins of 10 to 20 per cent. The Board accepted the ridiculous, gave the necessary instructions, and the losses were rapidly replaced by significant profits. The style of the Boardroom meetings determines the style of the company.

Apart from meetings of Directors, the Board is also responsible for calling General Meetings of members, or shareholders. The Annual General Meeting, or AGM, which must be within fifteen months of the last one, must cover:

- declaration of dividend;
- consideration and approval of the accounts, Directors' and auditor's reports;
- election of Directors, by rotation or appointed by the Board since the last General Meeting;
- appointment and remuneration of the auditors;
- any special business, such as altering the share capital, altering the Articles, approving the Directors' remuneration, incentive schemes and borrowing powers.

Shareholders who wish to remove any Directors must give special notice, twenty-eight days in advance of the General Meeting. This gives all those concerned a chance to prepare and circulate their case.

An Extraordinary General Meeting, or EGM, may be held if the Directors consider this is necessary, or if requested by 10 per cent of the shareholders. All business at an EGM is 'special business'.

Minutes of meetings

The Company Secretary records decisions taken at Board meetings, and drafts the minutes. These need only include decisions made, but it is sensible to add a brief record of the main factors, for and against, which led to their making. A decision, all on its own, can prove difficult to interpret after the passage of a little time.

The Chairman approves or amends the draft. Normal practice is that he then circulates his version to all Directors for their comments, usually in the bundle of papers for the next meeting. He obtains their approval, or occasional suggested amendments, at the beginning of that next meeting. He does not have to circulate the minutes, but is clearly wise to make this a routine. In meetings where there is a large measure of dissent, or where an item is complex, the best practice is for the Chairman to require the Company Secretary to draft the eventual decision at the meeting itself, while the Directors wait, and then have the wording agreed by all of them on the spot.

If any one Director believes that the draft minutes are
incorrect on any point, he must say so, and seek his co-
directors' agreement that the draft be amended. If they do not
agree, but he continues to judge that the matter is important,
he should ask that his disagreement also be recorded. Cabinet
ministers have often stated that they do not recognise the decisions recorded in the Cabinet minutes; company Directors frequently say the same. The fault is their own.

The Chairman signs the minutes of the meetings which he
chaired, and they are entered into a minute book. The 1948
Companies Act requires that there be such a book. This must
be a permanent record, and if in looseleaf format, each page
should be numbered and initialled.

The signed minutes become 'evidence' of the decisions
taken by the Board. Not 'conclusive evidence', unless the
Articles specifically state that they be 'conclusive'. In subsequent legal action it can be possible to demonstrate by other
means that additional decisions were taken by the Board, but
not minuted. The Director involved in such action will,
however, feel a little foolish that he has to find 'other means',
and did not ensure that the minutes were a proper record in
the first place.

The minute book is therefore a document of the greatest
importance. The Director of a company which is in trouble,
either in its external trading or in its internal behaviour, will
be wise to ensure that each month's minutes are a true and full
record of Board decisions, and that any strong objections he
has made are clearly recorded, if only to 'protect his back'. A
perfectly valid objective where there is a high level of
Boardroom conflict, or where internal behaviour is question-
able. If he does not take this precaution, who will believe him
anyway?

Minutes of General Meetings are normally signed at the
following Directors' meeting, to avoid leaving this till next
year's General Meeting.

Agenda and papers

The Board should plan its agenda three to four months ahead,
to give time for the production of specific papers by individual

Directors. Forward programmes should be minuted. If a scheduled paper will be delayed for some good reason, the Director concerned should inform his colleagues of this as soon as possible. They should not first learn about the delay at the meeting when the scheduled paper was due to be presented – they may be rushing some preparatory work of their own to meet that deadline.

All Directors should participate in the preparation of the forward agenda, particularly non-executives when they believe that questions of importance are either being ignored, or swept under the carpet. The non-executive may have a useful role to play outside the Boardroom, but it is within the Boardroom, in the agenda, and in the minuted decisions, where his primary contribution is evidenced – or not.

Papers should be short, opened by a summary of recommendations, then a summary of conclusions, then the body of hard facts or assumptions. The Director reading them has to be taken through the logic backwards. It is the bit on the front page that the presenting director has to justify. Papers should not be pre-vetted. The man responsible for the paper is responsible for deciding whom he will check it with in advance of circulation. It is not his boss's paper. It should give the Board a chance to judge his acuity, not his boss's.

Routines

When the Chief Executive draws up the job description for a newly-appointed manager he includes, among other things:

- the person's primary roles;
- his limits of authority in performing these roles; and
- the routines he is expected to maintain, monthly, quarterly, yearly.

This assists the Chief Executive to:

- check later that the manager is doing his job;
- guide the manager in planning his own activities;
- induce the manager to do regularly those things which he might otherwise let slip. Everyone lets slip the things they do not like doing.

So also with the Board. It draws up its own roles, and describes which Directors, or committees, do what in order to fulfil those roles. It defines the limits of each Director, or committee, and requires that anything beyond these limits be brought to the full Board. It can establish a programme of routines, including those things which it does not like doing, which describes what it will discuss and resolve, monthly, quarterly, half-yearly, yearly. For example:

Monthly

– Review of management and financial accounts, covering performance to date against the year's budget and recommendations for improvement. As with all reports, but particularly this one, it is essential that the Board describe in advance the desired content and extent of the subject matter. It needs enough, but not too much detail.
– Finance Director's report on cash and related matters.
– Chief Executive's report on operations, for review, decisions and recommendations. Again, enough, but not too much detail, otherwise the Board becomes a management committee.
– Business Development Director's report on trading situation, competition, overseas expansion, and similar. Many Boards rely on a single monthly report from the Chief Executive. This can place too much of the work, in detail, on one man's shoulders, and he may be of a character which is reluctant to be seen to share responsibilities. Better for the Board to decide in advance that instructions are channelled out of the Boardroom, and reports are therefore channelled back into the Boardroom, by the three separate key Directors; the Chief Executive, the Finance Director, and the Business Development Director. This does not subtract anything from the Chief Executive's ultimate operating responsibility. It just ensures that he does not try to do everything himself. Many do.

Quarterly

– A one-by-one divisional review, covering all of them once a year.
– A similar one-by-one functional review, covering all of

them once a year (personnel and training, marketing, production, research and development).
- Selected subsidiaries, including the critical ones and the best performers. Invite the MD to lunch afterwards; he may be nervous.

Half-yearly

- Industrial relations. It is hoped that this would not be necessary more frequently. Is the participation mechanism in good working order?
- Performance against long-term plans, not simply against budgets (which is checked monthly in the review of management accounts). Are the policies, objectives and strategies on beam? Is the organisational structure effective?
- Possibly a formal re-budgeting of critical subsidiaries or activities. The alteration of an approved one-year budget should only be agreed if the external environment has significantly changed, not if the managers are failing to perform to par. Maybe they ought to be altered instead.

Yearly

- Decision on, and communication of, any changes to corporate policies, objectives, or strategies.
- Approval of plans and budgets for the coming year.
- Annual performance review, with decisions on how improvements are to be effected.
- Annual review of senior staff performance below the Board, and whether any changes should be made.
- Annual Board review of its own performance as a Board, of the contribution of its individual Directors, particularly the non-executives, and of any changes it needs to make to the mix of Directors, skills and styles, in the Boardroom.
- Election, or re-election, of a Chairman.

Committees

There is no limitation on what the Board can choose to delegate to committees, but as it has to accept responsibility for the committees' actions and decisions, and therefore has to wade through the committees' reports, it is often just as effective, and at least as quick, to keep most of the deliberating and deciding within the full Board. The following are some of the most common committees.

Executive Committee

Many a UK (and US) Board is a facade behind which the real business of the company is controlled by an Executive Committee. Chaired by the Chief Executive, it contains two or three executive Directors and two or three non-Board managers, works entirely on its own initiatives, creates its own terms of reference, and receives little or no instruction or guidance from the Board. This practice can put the Board Directors at risk; it leaves them remote from the decisions and actions for which they ultimately carry the responsibility. This may not seem important when all is rosy; but will it ever be rosy again?

Establishing an Executive Committee can, nonetheless, be helpful to a Board which takes its responsibilities more seriously. The Board decides the areas to be covered and the kinds of actions to be taken; the Chief Executive takes away these guidelines from the Boardroom, disseminates them via his Executive Committee, and uses the Committee to decide on how to take the actions indicated.

The common assumption in the UK is that Executive Committees do not contain non-executives. In the US they are characteristically half executive, half non-executive. In 1974 the Securities and Exchange Commission in America required Mattel Inc, via a federal court order, to place a majority of non-executives on its Executive Committees. (It also required that the Board be entirely changed to introduce a majority of eight non-executives.) Similarly with Northrop Corporation which, following a 'class' action, had to appoint four new non-executives, and had to revive its Executive Committee with five or six non-executives. Its Nominating and Audit Committees had to be made entirely non-executive. In the UK, one or two non-executives on an Executive Committee should suffice.

Audit Committee

All companies with a New York Stock Exchange listing must have an Audit Committee with a majority of non-executives. (They must also have at least two non-executives to obtain a listing. The London Stock Exchange could helpfully introduce a similar ruling, but preferably with a minimum of three rather than two.) The NYSE definition of an independent outside Director, for Audit Committee purpose, is a Director who 'is independent of management and free from any relationship which could interfere with the exercise of independent judgement as a committee member'.

The Audit Committee in the US is intended:

(a)   to increase public confidence in the credibility and objectivity of published financial information;

(b)   to assist Directors in meeting their financial reporting responsibilities;

(c)   to strengthen the independent position of a company's external auditor by providing channels of communication between him and Directors other than the executives.

Managements may comment on any adverse conclusions tentatively reached by a US Audit Committee. (It is sensible policy in any context to let management comment on adverse conclusions regarding their behaviour or performance before the Board reacts to them.)

The Audit Committee:

- discusses problems with the auditors;
- discusses the effectiveness of internal financial controls, staffing, the EDP system – and recommends changes where these are found necessary;
- discusses the performance figures;
- checks on possible bribery, and on political contributions;
- approves, or not, the auditors.

In the UK, a Conservative Member of Parliament has tried several times to have a Bill enacted which would require UK companies to establish three-man teams of non-executives to

perform similar functions. The Accountants International
Study Group Report of 1977, and UK accounting institutions
in general, favour the establishment of such Audit Committees.

The question of charging an independent 'core' of the
Board to play this role has been accentuated in the UK by
Department of Trade reports on the failings of several one-
man dominated companies, and has been accentuated in the
US by a series of bribery and political contribution scandals.

But it will be readily apparent that management's cosy
relationship with the auditors, which the Audit Committee is
intended to prevent, could quite easily be replaced, after a
short passage of time, by a similarly cosy relationship between
the auditors and the Audit Committee – if the latter lets itself
become less than ruthless. The British are seldom ruthless for
very long.

Each reader may have his own view on the need, or not, for
Audit Committees. The writer (and the Institute of Directors)
believes they are not necessary, and that the Board should be
its own Audit Committee. It can only be this if it contains
enough non-executives who are truly impartial, truly 'critical',
truly pure-as-driven-snow – as well as being truly able to put
in the amount of time which a control activity of this kind
demands.

And thus we arrive, again, at the perpetual question of the
current UK, and US, practice of drawing non-executives from
that catchment area of full-time executives in other companies
who have demonstrated that they do not have, or do not spare,
the time. It can be considered a matter of shame that Boards
have had to have this committee imposed on them in the US,
and that the case for a similar committee can, sensibly, be
pressed so hard in the UK. The concept of the Audit Committee can only have grown in an environment where the
Directors, especially the non-executives, had demonstrated
that they were not playing their role with the commitment and
responsibility which it demands.

Remuneration or Compensation Committee

The predominantly or exclusively non-executive Remuneration or Compensation Committee determines the pay and per-

quisites of Directors and top managers. It is an 'obvious' committee, which avoids involving the executives in a hassle about each others' salaries, and although very common in the US, only one-third of UK Boards have one. More should.

As an aside, while the Committee will avoid the hassle, it will not be able to prevent the Directors learning what each is paid. In any group, dissent develops if rewards within the group are seen to be unreasonably different. If a Board has one executive on £20,000 and another on £45,000 – and it happens – then there is trouble afoot. The Committee should focus on forestalling such trouble.

Nominating Committee

The purpose of the Nominating Committee is to vet and present potential new Directors, especially non-executives. In the US half the Boards have one, and the proportion is increasing. In the UK there are very few.

The importance, and suggested composition, of this Committee has been argued in Chapter 9. The style and standard of contribution in Boardrooms could be greatly improved if a 'professional', methodical, semi-independent approach is made to recruiting Directors, instead of simply relying on, or surrendering to, the fancies of the Chairman or Chief Executive.

Finance Committee

One-third of US Boards have a Finance Committee, compared with one-sixth in the UK. They commonly include the Chairman, Chief Executive, finance Director, and one or two non-executives with financial or banking backgrounds. They commonly consider accounts, both half-year and full-year, and the proposed statements to cover the publication of those accounts; plus or minus the funding mix, the appointment of bankers and financial advisers, and the implications of the cash flow forecasts.

All these activities are so fundamental to the overall deliberations of the Board as a whole that it can be argued that they are best left to the full Board.

Planning Committee

About one in seven of the larger UK companies have Planning Committees. It is doubtful whether one in seven of the smaller or medium-sized companies even have a planning office anywhere within their organisation.

Companywide planning, leading on the one hand to very detailed subsidiary company plans, and on the other hand to resources-oriented collective corporate plans, needs onerous explanation, exhortation and coordination. It is recommended that the Business Development Director be charged by the Board with establishing and chairing a committee to undertake this most vital activity; drawing up formats, defining and explaining contents, assisting with compilation, illustrating how Group policies affect the individual units, highlighting the possible, eliminating the fantastic, organising the annual country-house planning weekend, collating and presenting the finalised whole to the Board for approval.

The Board, it is repeated, has no more important managerial role than to initiate and maintain a clockwork planning routine which carries through all the company's thinking. Planning is a way of thinking, an attitude of mind.

Other Committees

Other committees may be set up as the Board judges helpful. For example, a Donations and Charities Committee may seem a nuisance for those who are press-ganged, but it does eliminate some of the Chairman's pet causes which have no corporate relevance. Establish a Committee of two, the Company Secretary and one non-executive. Give it two hours one wet afternoon; define how much each subsidiary can spend, and how much the corporate centre can spend. Instruct all units that they must clear proposed payments centrally with the Company Secretary before making them – there may be some overlaps which can be eliminated this way. Give him discretion up to a contingency of 10 per cent of the total – it will be consumed in the first month of the year. Then let him tell everyone else who approaches him that 'sorry, the budget is overspent', which will be true. Otherwise the whole business gets out of hand; otherwise the Directors will spend more time arguing about £50 for the Retired Lozenge Wrappers Benevolent Fund than they will on £500,000 for the new factory in Bootle.

A Personnel/Training/Management Development Committee may be set up for a year or so, if the Board decides it has neglected these areas. Once routines are established, the Committee can be disbanded, and these matters then slot into a quarterly or half-yearly spot on the agenda.

Other committees used in the UK and US are recorded in Appendix I. The lists are not exhaustive; one major US corporation also has an Operations Committee as well as a Technology and Science Committee. Others have a PR Committee, Sealing Committee and Stock Transfer Committee.

Be guided, when considering whether to establish a committee or not, by the fact that all committees, apart from the Audit and Executive Committees, can basically only help by digesting a welter of detail, and then presenting a pre-digested, slimmed-down version to the full Board. If the Board really needs all the detail to reach a firm, responsible conclusion, it does not need a committee.

Dissent; resignation; removal

The Board decides by a majority of the Directors. A Director who disagrees with the decision of the majority will normally accept it, and help to implement it, but if his disagreement is very strong, either because he believes the decision will lead the company into serious trouble, or because he believes it is not wholly in accordance with the law, he has to express and press his dissent.

He can, and should, have his dissent minuted against his name.

He can call a special Board meeting to discuss his dissent, but there is no guarantee that any of the other directors will come to it.

He can circulate his co-directors with his views if he feels they were not given a good airing (which may have been his own fault).

And if he has convinced himself that he is not just being 'contrary', and that what he complains about really is foolish, illegal, corrupt or immoral, he can arrange to put his case to a General Meeting of shareholders, in the form of a resolution of no confidence in the policy of the Board. The shareholders cannot reverse any decision taken by the Board, nor can they instruct the Board on any matter which the Board is empowered by the articles to decide, but the shareholders can, if they agree with the dissenting Director, choose to remove the rest of the Directors.

He can also propose to the General Meeting that they request that a Department of Trade Inspector be put into the company.

Or, as an alternative to the usually destructive weapon of a general meeting resolution, and dependent on the exact nature of his concern, he might threaten his colleagues with a chat with the auditors, or with the company's bankers. This can be a practical alternative in a private company where the main shareholders are also on the Board.

But he cannot remain quiet. In the Department of Trade Inspector's Report on First Re-Investment Trust Ltd, all the Directors were castigated in varying degrees for not having stopped a dominant Chairman who was doing what he should not. Some of these Directors had in fact 'complained'. But not enough to rid them of all responsibility.

He might consider court action, if he is also a shareholder. But only if he believes the Board is acting fraudulently, or ultra vires. Better to use the General Meeting, and leave it to them to decide whether to use the court.

He can resign. He must do so if the Board is acting illegally, and will not remedy its illegal actions. If he does so, he should explain, publicly, why he is doing so. Otherwise no lessons will be learnt, and the company will almost certainly be harmed, not helped. Resignation must be written, or verbal at a General Meeting. It cannot be withdrawn, even if it has not been formally accepted.

He might get himself removed. Normally a Board cannot remove a Director before the expiry of his term of office, unless the articles say it can. They usually do not say this, and Table A has no relevant provision.

The Board might lobby friendly shareholders to remove him, and they can at any time, given due notice under the special notice rules. In this instance the Director concerned has the right to circulate a written statement of his case, and present it at the relevant general meeting. This might do the trick.

The Board might seduce him to go quietly with a large golden handshake. (They might do that, also, if he is patently 'wrong', not 'right'.) This might prove counter-productive; the level of handshake being paid is already causing some disgust among laymen and other Directors. Shareholders do not always query the why and the why-so-much to the extent that the average layman would expect. Shareholders might do a lot more to look after their own interests.

11   Dos and don'ts for Directors

The Board has to decide policies, generate plans, appoint management and hold it responsible – in the interests of the company as a whole. It can only do this effectively when it is composed and led in a way which requires each Director to work purposefully towards that objective, without influence from specialist interests, dominant interests within the Boardroom, or self-interest. Therefore:

DO propose and pursue the composing of a Board which

- is chaired by an independent director who is not also managing the company;
- is business-oriented, not figures- nor technology-oriented alone;
- contains a core of executives including a Chief Executive, who is people-oriented rather than figures- or technology-oriented, alone, plus a Finance Director and a Business Development Director; contains a balance of part-time non-executives with very varied skills and styles, half of them executive Directors in other companies, half of them from among Board-experienced consultants, academics and professional directors who provide added width and depth;
- has the maturity of judgement to be able to make productive use of the occasional conflict of strong opinions.

DO ensure that

- the Board formally reviews its composition and performance, as a Board, once each year;
- the changes to the mix of membership, or to the terms of

reference of existing members, are agreed at that formal meeting;
- the terms of reference for new Directors are matched to the needs of the Board and of the company, not to the wishes of any one Director or interest grouping;
- the Chairman of the Board is elected or re-elected at that meeting, election being based on the criterion of who is best able to perform the role, not of maintaining status or status quo, alone.

DO require a minimum commitment of two days per month from each non-executive and arrange that some of them overlap onto lower Boards, and onto joint-venture and associate company Boards, if you have such within the Group. This improves the Board's vision, understanding and control.

To enable the Board to remain, collectively, in control:

DO ensure that the Board

- collectively compiles its forward agenda;
- maps out a programme of routines for monthly, quarterly, half-yearly and yearly reviews, so that all functional and line activities are, and are seen by the company to be, regularly evaluated by the Board;
- meets 10–12 times each year;
- calls for and coordinates papers to a defined timetable, so that meetings do not become a shambles;
- establishes some, but not too many, Board committees to smooth the mechanics of the Boardroom – especially nominating, remuneration and planning committees;
- decides and communicates company policies;
- maintains formal business planning, allocating resources against a required scale and time-scale of returns;
- considers plans for overseas expansion as a priority (the UK population is 2 per cent of the world's total; markets are people);
- maintains a clockwork system for communication and participation which parallels the company's control structure;
- reviews once or twice annually the company's control

structure, amending it in step with changes in the company's growth. Remember that almost every company leaves structural change too late to avoid people-problems, which are always more onerous than marketing or methods problems;

- defines limits of authority for senior staff and individual units;
- operates as far as possible through largely autonomous divisions and subsidiaries, working within their limits and containing a mix of executives, Group executives and non-executives on their own Boards who can ensure that they do not run astray;
- monitors management against budgets; assists where there is a short-fall; then changes management if it still performs below par;
- maintains a routine of cash monitoring in each unit, each day.

When you sense that problems are developing:

DO study the characteristics of companies which collapse (Chapter 8), apprise the Board, initiate a time-scaled programme of remedial action. Always put 'actions' into the minutes, and 'time-scales' into the actions. Remember 'luck' rarely comes into it; bad results mean bad management, means a bad Board.

DO stimulate the Board or, through the Board, any lower level to engage defined-term doses of outside expertise. Something else which most companies leave late – and some too late.

And always:

DO make better use of those external organisations which benefit from the survival of your company:

- your bankers (they do well on your overdraft, could and would be helpful in many ways, but are strangely shy of volunteering suggestions);
- your main institutional shareholders (they know how others view your company, which may be nearer reality than your own viewpoint);

- your industrial associations and spokesbodies (they are only as good as the guidance they receive from member companies).

DO meet external responsibilities to time, as a habit. Delay does not remove debt, and it may only disguise the depth of the hole down which you are continuing to fall.

DO read your company's Memorandum and Articles, and the Companies Acts of 1948, 1967, 1976 and 1980. Regularly. Ask the Company Secretary to circulate copies. You may get some surprises.

DO keep the Board well within the limits of all the laws, and keep morality a notch above legality.

DO keep at the front of your mind that:

- your are responsible to the company. If the company prospers, so do the employees, shareholders, creditors, Chairman and Chief Executive;
- you are supposed to ask 'searching questions';
- the Board is a 'group', and groups thrive on diversity, stagnate under conformity, and suffocate under domination.

Each Director is just one vote. Each vote can be a helpful voice, or a hollow echo of some more dominant voice. When a Board is dominated by a Chairman or Chief Executive it can be very difficult for the individual Director to find his voice. When a Board contains no truly independent, or no truly committed, non-executives, it can become impossible. Therefore:

DON'T allow the Board to be dominated. Lobby your colleagues, prepare a combined case, present it diplomatically outside the Boardroom. If this does not do the trick, vote in combination in the Boardroom to effect a change or two. You, too, may have to bully. You may lose the case. You may feel you have to quit. As a Director, you are responsible to the company, not to your career. That's the 'consideration' you pay for joining the Board of a Company Limited. But if you do not play the Director's role responsibly, and with courage, how can you expect a lathe operator to give a damn, either?

DON'T vote for a combined Chairman/Chief Executive. That is what often creates the problem in the first place.

DON'T let the Chairman do everything. Don't let him do very much. The role of Chairman is the most important position in commerce and industry. The Chairman is Chairman of the Board. But he is not Chairman of the company. There is no such position as Chairman of the company.

DON'T vote for a new Chairman who is at present Chief Executive. The roles are entirely different. The characteristics and personalities required are mutually exclusive.

DON'T let the Chairman decide who will be the next Chief Executive. He may propose someone he can man-handle. Or he may indeed propose the best man – but the Board as a whole decides.

DON'T elect a Chief Executive who does not carry the votes of all, or of almost all the executive Directors. The non-executives may be in a majority on the Board, but if there is such strong disagreement about an internal candidate there must be good enough reasons – so the non-executives should call for external candidates to be considered.

DON'T elect joint MDs, except just occasionally in the largest Holding Boards where the men head divisions which are quite discrete.

DON'T elect managers to be executive Directors as a reward for being good managers, when they are not able to contribute productively to most items on the agenda. If they are really valuable managers, give them a much better remuneration package to demonstrate they are valued.

DON'T appoint or promote anyone to the Board as an executive Director without applying a professional recruitment process, including a Board committee, advertising the position, obtaining support from a recruitment consultant, psychological testing, full Board vetting. Don't leave 99 per cent of this key responsibility in the hands of a head hunter, alone, even if you choose to use one, also. Don't use head hunting in countries where it is not wholly sanctioned by the local laws.

DON'T appoint non-executives who are retired executives from your company. They cannot be truly independent. Nor retired executives from any other company unless they retired early to become professional Directors.

DON'T appoint non-executives who represent specialist interests, e.g. consumers, employees, unions, ethnic minorities, sexes. Just appoint 'contributors'.

DON'T appoint non-executives because they are your bankers, lawyers, business associates of any kind, nor members of 'the family'. Nor civil servants (retired), admirals (retired), lords, MPs, big names who are happy to passively make weight. Nor chums. Nor anyone who cannot give your company a minimum of two days per month, and more when you really need it. Directorship is more serious, more responsible, more critically important than a short sharp trot through a bundle of monthly papers.

DON'T be afraid of the maverick, the court jester, the critical Director, the uncomfortable Director. They are performing what the role entails, their way. And they are performing.

DON'T apply any qualifications to Board membership which have nothing to do with business performance, e.g. schooling, clubs, religion, freemasonry, nationality, natural tendencies. Many do.

DON'T let Humphrey leave, again, before item 4. Or William doze off, again, before item 3. If that really is the best they can do, it is not good enough.

DON'T agree to Associate or Alternate Directors. There are better alternatives.

DON'T give inflated golden handshakes when you have to part company with an executive. Soon enough that grossly abused practice will stimulate even the shareholders to complain. What are you actually paying for, and why do you have to? Should he be paying you something?

DON'T let the Board spend longer on choosing pictures for the corridor than on choosing a site for the new factory. If you tease the Chairman once or twice he will take the message.

DON'T, ever, let a vote go by on the nod when you disagree. Say you disagree. You do not have to make a big issue out of every second-order item, but your voice might trigger two or three others who also disagree, and together you might develop a conclusion which moves the company forward, even if only a little. The 'silly' question or silly comment is seldom as silly as you think it may sound.

Regarding the company itself:

DON'T get involved in restrictive trade practices, such as collusive bidding. It only helps to hide bad management, or bad marketing, and only slightly prolongs the time that these inadequacies can be hidden. After which time the damage to your company will have increased.

DON'T maltreat your environment with effluent, noise, or ugliness. But don't, either, get charity-minded. The need for charity in your community is greater than your company can handle.

DON'T create or maintain:

- subsidiaries just to create directorships;
- funnies;
- minorities in your subsidiaries if you can buy them out;
- associate companies, unless their ROC is markedly greater than that of your subsidiaries;
- joint ventures, unless essential, for example overseas;
- any subsidiary, division, committee or other organisation which does not have clear terms of reference and measured and time-scaled objectives, which it has a reasonable chance of meeting.

DON'T leave the Chief Executive to chair the Divisional or Subsidiary Boards. Use non-executives.

DON'T leave the linking of the Board and the shopfloor to a one-man chain of Chief Executive and direct line subordinates. Use multiple linkages for better communication, better control. 'Control' is not solely a line-management matter. The Chief Executive and his managers control operations. The Board needs to control how well its policies, objectives, plans are attuned to the company's needs and abilities. These are not exclusively line-management matters.

DON'T forget, however difficult this may occasionally be:

- you are responsible to the company;
- you have to analyse it, plan it, structure it, ensure that it is properly managed;
- where it is less than perfect, you have to do something about it.

That is why you are ON THE BOARD.

Appendix I
Composition of unitary Boards in the UK, USA and Japan

This appendix contains a summary of data on unitary, or single-tier, Boards in the UK and USA, against which the reader can compare his own Board's composition, and his own ideas as to how its membership might be improved. These are 'status quo' data, and do not represent 'ideals'.

Notes on Japanese unitary Boards are also included, as an aside. The culture, history and environment in which Japanese companies have evolved are so different from those of the UK, Europe and the US that, while comparisons are thought-provoking, they cannot in themselves be very productive.

UK Boards

The following figures are either extracted directly from the sources acknowledged, or are an amalgam and rounding where the sources have varied slightly through having drawn on differing samples.

Three ranges of company size are postulated:

(a) the largest 200 or so public companies in the *Times 1000*;
(b) the middle section of the *Times 1000*;
(c) private companies with up to 500 employees, or up to £5 million turnover.

1 Board size:

   (a) 5–20+ Directors, average 12, 50 per cent with
        11–15, 25 per cent over 16;
   (b) 4–16 Directors, average 9, 80 per cent with 6–10, 7
        per cent over 10;
   (c) 2–10 Directors, average and majority at 5–6.

2 Non-executives:

   (a) 33 per cent of total, on average 4, 10 per cent of
        these largest companies have none;
   (b) 33 per cent of total, average 3, nearly 30 per cent
        have none (contrary to the Korn/Ferry and Booz
        Allen surveys, a Bank of England study concluded
        that only 12 per cent had none);
   (c) 20 per cent of total, average 1, 46 per cent have none
        (Booz Allen survey, 1979 – a BIM study in 1970
        found that only 20 per cent of this category had
        none).

3 Combined Chairman/Chief Executive:

   (a) 50 per cent of companies in this category combine
        the two roles. In 80 per cent of them the Chairman
        has some executive functions;
   (b) 45 per cent of companies combine these two roles.
        In 60 per cent of them the Chairman has some
        executive functions;
   (c) 69 per cent of companies have 'Executive Chair-
        men'.

4 Time committed by non-executives:

   This averages around one day per month in all
   categories, though varying from well under 6 days per
   year to over 25 days per year.

5 Number of Board meetings:

   Most companies have 8–11 Board meetings per year.
   Some hold just 1, some 24.

6 In the 308 *Times 1000* companies in the Korn/Ferry
   survey, the backgrounds of the non-executives were found

to be:

Chairman (in another company)	210
Managing Director	141
Finance Director	86
Marketing Director	31
Production Director	22
Sales Director	5
Personnel Director	5
Vice-chairman	3
Deputy managing Director	1

504 non-executives from a total of 965, or 52 per cent, were found to be Directors in other companies. This contrasts with Booz Allen survey results, which found that while over 50 per cent of non-executives in the UK are employed full time elsewhere, only 25 per cent are executive Directors in other companies.

Previous employees	95
Law	75
Shareholder	73
Banking	54
Accounting	48
Politics	28
Retired executives	26
Government	18
Stockbrokers	8
(Other)	8
Academics	7
Landowners	5
Civil servants	5
Diplomats	3
Professional non-executives	3
Auditor's representative	1
Management consultant	1
Medical	1
Trade union	1

It is not known what percentage of these categories is

working full time elsewhere, and what percentage is above normal retiring age, though 26 per cent, or 12.5 per cent of all non-executives, are shown as 'previous employees' or 'retired executives'. This also contrasts with the Booz Allen survey results, which found that 21–43 per cent of all non-executives were 'retired' from full-time employment.

The Korn/Ferry survey found that only 61 per cent of the smaller companies in the *Times 1000* would allow their executives to be non-executives in other companies, and only 29 per cent of this category would allow them to retain the non-executive fees which they earned, the rest having to pay these into their employing companies. A 'mean' practice, given the extra work? For the largest companies, the respective figures were 97 and 69 per cent.

7   The main sources for introducing non-executives to a company were stated to be:

> by the Chairman, 40–50 per cent, the higher figure in the largest companies;
> by other Directors, 30 per cent;
> by shareholders, 2–15 per cent;
> by advisers, 4–12 per cent.

Nominating committees (0–7 per cent) and 'search' or head hunting (1–4 per cent) play a surprisingly small role.

8   Over 50 per cent of non-executives have served for more than five years.

9   The majority of companies, in all categories, believe that the importance of the non-executive role is increasing.

10 In the 308 *Times 1000* companies in the Korn/Ferry survey, the executive Directors comprise:

Managing Director	332
Divisional Director	300
Finance Director	284 – i.e. 8 per cent do
Chairman	216 not have one

Marketing Director	138	– i.e. 55 per cent do
Production Director	116	not have one
Sales Director	94	
Personnel Director	92	– frequency increas-
Planning/Administration	30	ing with increasing
Legal/Company secretary	25	size of company
Deputy Managing Director	23	
(Other)	23	
Vice-chairman	21	
Technical Director	21	
Property Director	16	
Regional/Territorial	16	
Product Director	14	
Purchasing Director	13	
R & D Director	13	
Engineering Director	7	
Operations Director	7	
Distribution Director	6	
PR Director	5	
Retail Director	4	
Management services Director	2	
Service Director	1	
Overseas Director	1	

11   The BIM survey of small to medium-sized private companies in 1970 found that:

> 62–79 per cent had marketing/sales Directors;
> 67–68 per cent had production/R & D Directors;
> 37–46 per cent had finance Directors;
> 16–30 per cent had legal/secretarial Directors;
> 19–23 per cent had purchasing Directors;
> 17–18 per cent had technical/engineering Directors; and
> 16–18 per cent had personnel/training Directors.

12   The Board committees established by the 308 companies in the Korn/Ferry sample include:

Executive	125
Remuneration	111 = 36 per cent

Finance	56
Planning	42 = 14 per cent
Audit	40
Personnel	25
Nominating	10 = 3 per cent
Policy	6
Chairman's	6
Subsidiary	3
Pension fund	2
Property	2
Charities	2
General purpose	2
Share option	2

USA Boards

The historical development of American corporations has differed from that of UK companies, partly as a result of differing State legislation regarding incorporation, partly through the early usage of the 'limited partnership', borrowed from Europe, which substituted for the 'private company' concept of the UK. With time visible practice has drawn closer, though still differs to a marked degree in the extent to which Directors in America are brought to face their legal liabilities in court actions.

The following data are taken from a Korn/Ferry survey in 1980 of 552 corporations. Nearly all of these are 'large' or 'very large' by UK standards, and the data are hereunder split between:

(a)   corporations with turnover above $200 million;

(b)   corporations with turnover below $200 million.

1   Board size:

(a)   average 13 – where turnover exceeds $5 billion average is 16, with insurance companies average is 16, with banks and financial institutions average is 19;

(b)   average 9.

2   Non-executives:

  (a)   average 9 out of 13 – where turnover exceeds $5 billion 10/16, with insurance companies 12/16, with banks and financial institutions 15/19;
  (b)   average 6 out of 9.

Boards have a clear, and increasing, preference for a large non-executive majority, but executives may disagree (see Chapter 6, 'The professional Director').

3   Combined Chairman/Chief Executive Officer:
    72 per cent of the corporations in the sample combine these two roles; where turnover exceeded $5 billion the figure is 93 per cent.

4   Time committed by non-executives:

  (a)   average 105 hours per year, equivalent to 13 days, or 1 day per month;
  (b)   average 78 hours per year, or 9–10 days, well under 1 day per month.

In corporations with turnover above $1 billion the average contribution is 75 per cent higher than that given in smaller corporations, which parallels experience in the UK. But even in these largest corporations the average does not exceed 18–19 days per year, or 1.5 days per month.

Contribution exceeds 20 days per year in less than 9 per cent of all corporations, and is less than 1 day per month in fully 75 per cent of all corporations which responded to this question. As we can safely assume that a large number of the 15 per cent of corporations which did not answer this question were in fact ashamed to do so, the average contribution must be well below even these striking figures. And they are 'striking figures' when we take into account that US Boards are predominantly non-executive, and that such a high proportion have combined Chairmen/CEOs. It cannot be surprising that there is widespread concern in the US regarding the performance of Directors, and in this connection the reader's attention is drawn to 6, below.

5   Number of Board meetings:

> average 8 per year – 33 per cent had 10–12 per
> annum; 41 per cent had 5–9; 20 per cent had less
> than 5.

6   Background of non-executives:

> The proportion of Boards containing non-executives
> with the backgrounds listed is shown for1973 and
> 1979, to illustrate trends:

	% 1973	% 1979
Senior executive from another company	85.3	88.4
Retired executive or previously employed executive	55.7	55.8
Academic	34.9	51.6
Commercial banker	55.4	43.1
Female	10.7	36.4
Attorney – serving company	51.7	35.1
Stockholder – but not officer	43.1	32.2
Attorney – not serving company	n/a	32.1
Investment banker	37.3	28.3
Former government official	14.4	23.2
Ethnic minority representative	8.9	19.2
Non-US citizen	n/a	16.7
US international executive	n/a	11.4
Employee representative	n/a	2.2
Consumer group representative	n/a	2.0

7   The main sources for introducing non-executives to a
company were stated to be:

	%	
Chairman	78	
Other Directors	80	
Other officers	54	
Nominating committee	46	(increasing)
Executive acquaintances	24	
'Search' or head-hunting	8	(slightly increasing)
Banker	1	
Attorney	1	

8   Board committees:

	% of companies which have	average number of meetings per annum	executive/ non-executive
Audit*	99	4	0/4
Compensation	90	4	0/4
Executive	81	6	3/3
Nominating	47	2	1/4
Finance	32	7	2/4
Public affairs	10	3	1/4
Corporate ethics	7	2	1/3

*All companies listed on NYSE must have.

Japanese Boards

There are four categories of Japanese company, the predominant type resembling the limited liability company of the UK.

Boards contain from 5–30+ Directors, commonly 14–16. They are thus much larger than UK Boards, and slightly larger than those of US corporations. A unique feature is that the Boards appoint two or three of their number to be 'representative Directors', who represent the company to third parties, and who sign for it.

All Directors are elected at general meetings of shareholders. This is normally through proxies vested in the Board, so that membership of the Board is in practice controlled by the management. As few as 3 per cent of the shareholders can request the court to remove a Director they judge to be inadequate, and a majority of only two-thirds of the shareholders can alter the articles under which the Directors operate (compared with the 75 per cent majority required in the UK).

However, the position of the small shareholder is much weaker than this might suggest. Changes to the Commercial Code during the post-World War II military occupation, when the giant 'zaibatsus' were broken up, may have been intended to increase the power of the shareholders, but in practice had the opposite effect. While before the war there were numerous part-time non-executives on Japanese Boards, today there are few indeed – around 1 in 30 Directors only, having a role equivalent to the 'independent outsider' on UK or US Boards. Japanese executive Boards are still able to resist any change to their unhindered control of their own operations.

Abuse of this position has extended to the employment of 'sokaiya', or sophisticated toughs, whose role is to cut short any shareholder who complains too much at general meetings. Japanese police estimate that there are around 5,000 sokaiya in the country, and that 3,000 listed Japanese companies pay out close to £100 million per annum to these toughs to perform that role. Corrupt practice of any kind tends to rebound on the user of the practice, and the sokaiya discovered that they could maintain their high fee rates by threatening to blackmail companies, or individual Directors, who would not pay. The sokaiya have established networks within companies which keep them supplied with details of the darker deeds of the Directors; this they have been able to hold over the heads of the Boards concerned. Recently 1,000 or so of the listed companies decided to resist such blackmail, and enlisted the aid of the police, though the influence of the sokaiya has yet to be eliminated.

The small shareholder owns just over 30 per cent of the equity of listed companies, which is roughly the same proportion as is held by individual shareholders in the UK. But the composition of the larger shareholders is very different in the two countries. While pension funds and insurance companies do hold sizeable stakes in Japanese companies, the majorities are held by the companies' own bankers, and by trading or other companies with which there are close business relationships. Thus meetings of shareholders are in a sense 'family affairs', and even here the 'collective' character of Japanese enterprise is well demonstrated. The dominant shareholders are much more interested in business cooperation, on a continuing basis, than they are in dividends or capital gains.

The executive Board is thus free from 'pressure' from the

shareholders. Until 1974 it was also effectively free from any real pressure from its auditors, who were considered till then to be subordinate to the management, and often consisted of unqualified retired Directors, or trainees who were being groomed for a directorship – the very last categories to complain about management's performance, or its treatment of its accounts.

In 1974 an Act was passed introducing statutory auditors, elected by the general meeting and reporting to it. They were given increased powers. On the evidence to date, these are about as passive as their predecessors. While they are not allowed to be Directors or managers, it is reported that they are commonly treated as normal employees, within a hierarchy. The Board continues to be allowed to be strongly self-protective.

Entry to the Board is controlled by the Chairman, the president, and perhaps one other senior Director, who may or may not take external advice, for example from the bankers, before promoting a manager to a directorship. With a strictly executive Board, directorship is seen as one more rung up the management ladder, not as a wholly separate role. Within the Board there is also a pronounced hierarchy, from the Chairman of the Board (most frequently a retired president) through the president of the corporation, to executive vice-president, senior MDs, MDs, to senior and then junior 'ordinary' Directors. These are not legally-defined positions, but the terms are commonly used.

Junior Directors will never rock the boat, and will never criticise a senior Director, even when he is patently 'wrong'. All levels of Director fear the loss of face implicit in a sideways move to some ceremonial role, and will not risk it. The wishes of senior Directors therefore always prevail.

Executive committees, and committees of managing Directors are also used, and meet frequently, often weekly.

The nearest one normally finds to the 'non-executive' role is in the frequent use of advisers to top management, who work alongside, but outside, the Board. They are often retired executives.

While managers and other employees retire at 55 years, there is no retiring age for the Board. A small number of companies have recently introduced their own internal rules for retirement of Directors, but there is no evidence of haste to adopt the practice as a norm. The Chairman generally goes on for as long as he himself chooses.

Power within the Boardroom tends to be concentrated in the hands of two or three top Directors, with little or no check on their performance. But then Japanese companies, through all levels and activities, are concerned with the performance of groupings, not with the performance of individual men. The whole structure of a Japanese company is made up of numerous groups, which can be shaped and re-shaped as the immediate needs of the company change. A company structure chart will illustrate these groupings, and will include the title of the group leader, but not his name. The individual manager will not have a job description. His status will be defined by a level, but not by a job. He can be moved about sideways, and frequently is.

The Japanese believe that all tasks must be carried out by groups, and that success lies in the success of the group in achieving the tasks set for it. This may depend to some extent on the skill of the (temporary) leader of the group in eliciting maximum performance, but the success will not be attributed to him individually. This characteristic recognition of the importance of group decision making, and the strong task- and goal-orientation of Japanese groups, will remind the reader of the findings on group effectiveness which were recorded in Chapter 1. It has given the Japanese company great flexibility and mobility, which have in turn helped it to meet crises, or external business challenge. Coupled with the 'ringi' system, in which all who are able to contribute to a business decision are closely involved at all levels and stages, this has given the Japanese company a commitment to decisions finally made, and thus a concerted drive, which other competing countries have not been able to match. But it has been based on the inborn sense of collective responsibility which is found in Japan all the way from the quasi-kinship relationships of the village to the dealings of a corporation with its bankers, trading partners and government.

It does introduce problems as the zaibatsus re-group, as the size of individual corporations increases, and as structural fragmentation, which results from multi-group operation, becomes less easily managed. Some Japanese companies are trying to modernise their structures with western-style divisionalisation. One has even skipped over the ringi system in taking a major, and necessarily rapid, decision – C. Itoh and Co. when, in cooperation with Sumitomo Bank, it took over the failing Ataka and Co.

Two other weaknesses will need to be overcome. Firstly, the concept of general management, of total line management authority being vested in one man, is still alien to the Japanese. Groupings of senior executives normally carry out functions which, in the UK or US, would be delegated to a Chief Executive, even in down-line companies. This can slow action and reaction. Secondly, each corporation contains a series of parallel, vertical hierarchies, or 'habatsus', made up of cliques related by common schooling, common university, or some other similarly shared background. Bonds within these cliques are strong, and a man often works his way up through the organisation by being promoted through the good offices of his clique-colleagues above him. This system criss-crosses with the horizontal, task-oriented groupings, and sometimes causes destructive conflict. Such conflict has, to date, been held to a minimum by focusing the attention of the groupings on beating some further afield target, such as selected foreign competitors.

Stresses are actively developing within Japanese companies, stimulated by the disruptions of the 1970s when the proportion of the national import bill made up of oil was pushed to 37 per cent. Change will come, and will steadily absorb some of the most effective characteristics of western organisation. But it will come slowly. Boards and senior managements can still protect their individual positions. And the Bushido concepts of self-renunciation and obedience to superiors are still very strong.

Appendix II
Two-tier Boards in West Germany, Denmark and France

In the autumn of 1979 the Legal Affairs Committee of the European Parliament rejected, by 13 votes to 9, the European Commission's proposal for the appointment of worker Directors to company Boards in the EEC member countries. British Conservative members of the committee, who had been joined in this vote by the Liberals and Christian Democrats, stated then that it was vital that any proposals for a common format throughout the EEC 'shall represent a fair compromise of the essential features acceptable in the member States and should not blindly follow the German form of company organisation'.

It will be seen by comparing the following outline of current West German company organisation with alternative two-tier systems, such as those of Denmark and France, and then by comparing any one of these with the unitary Board system of the UK, that a compromise which really does include the 'essential features' of all of them will not be possible. Nor necessary; nor desirable.

West German Boards

The West German two-tier system evolved without disharmony from its introduction by Bismarck over a hundred years ago till the Codetermination Act (*Mitbestimmungsgesetz*) of 1976. Employer organisations instituted legal proceedings in the German constitutional court to have this Act declared

215

unconstitutional, though pending resolution of this major disharmony the Act remains in force. Its main provisions are as follows.

1 A private limited company (*Gesellschaft mit beschränkter Haftung*, GmbH) with less than 500 employees may retain a single-tier Board, with shareholder-elected Directors alone, unless the company and the employees voluntarily agree that they want a two-tier structure and worker Directors. There are 150,000 GmbH in Germany, compared with 2,500 public limited companies (AG). Most maintain the single tier, in which the manager (*Geschäftsführer*) or managers are appointed by a general meeting, or specifically by the articles. The shareholders may give instructions to the managers at meetings, or if the managers are not also members, outside of meetings. Managers must act jointly unless the articles allow (as they normally do) sole action, or dual action by two managers or one manager and a procuration holder (*Prokurist*).

2 Non-business organisations, such as political, religious, charitable, educational, artistic or opinion-disseminating groupings may also maintain a single-tier structure.

3 A GmbH with more than 500 employees, and any public limited company (*Aktiengesellschaft*, AG) outside of the mining, iron and steel industries must adopt the two-tier structure. The supervisory Board (*Aufsichtsrat*) appoints or removes members of, and supervises, the management Board (*Vorstand*), determines their remuneration, and can reduce such remuneration in times of severe financial stress, irrespective of existing contracts. It determines company policy, but cannot manage, nor represent the company to third parties. It receives regular reports from the management Board on performance, trading, problems, and related, and can request information at any time from the management Board on matters it considers of importance. It can specify

which transactions, or types of transaction, require its prior consent. The management Board manages the company, represents the company to third parties, and is bound by resolutions of the supervisory Board, though not by resolutions of a general meeting. Members of the management Board may not become members of Boards of other companies without permission. In companies with between 500 and 2,000 employees the supervisory Board contains from 3–21 Directors, dependent on the size of the company's capital, the total being required to be divisible by three. Two-thirds are shareholder representatives (often bankers, in larger companies) and one-third are employee representatives elected by ballot of the employees. One or two of the employee representatives must be actual employees of the company. A person cannot be a member of a supervisory Board if he is already a member of 10 other supervisory Boards, nor if he is a member of the management Board or the Board of one of the company's subsidiaries.

4 More complex rules apply to companies with more than 2,000 employees, which explains why many larger corporations are seeking to reorganise into visibly smaller units. There are around 1,000 companies in this size category. Half of the Directors are shareholder representatives, half are employee representatives:

   (i) for 2,000–10,000 employee companies, there must be 12 Directors – 6 representative of shareholders, 4 employees, 2 union nominees;

  (ii) for 10,000–20,000 employee companies, there must be 16 Directors – 8 representing shareholders, 6 employees, 2 union nominees;

(iii) above 20,000 there must be 20 Directors – 10 representing shareholders, 7 employees, 3 union nominees.

The rules require that 'employee' representation

include wage-earning 'blue-collar' men, salaried 'white-collar' men, and executive staff. All companies with more than 2,000 employees, and all companies in the mining, iron and steel industries, irrespective of size, must have a labour Director (*Arbeitsdirektor*). He is appointed by the shareholders, but he cannot be removed against the votes of the employee representatives on the supervisory Board. Despite the apparent arithmetic, the shareholders maintain a marginal advantage in companies with more than 2,000 employees. The Chairman has a casting vote. He is elected by the members of the supervisory Board by a two-thirds majority, or by a simple majority if two-thirds is not attained. If no simple majority can be attained either, then the Chairman is elected solely by the 'shareholder' Directors, and the vice-chairman, who has no casting vote, is elected by the employee Directors. This marginal advantage extends also in theory to the appointment of the management Board, which is again by a two-thirds majority or, failing that, by a simple majority.

Note: the 'exoneration', or relief (*Entlastung*) of both the supervisory and management Boards is decided annually in general meeting. It is intended to signify confidence, but it does not provide any waiver of liability.

5 Companies in the mining, iron and steel industries are governed by a separate set of very complex rules. Broadly, they have supervisory Boards with 11–21 members; equal numbers of shareholder and employee Directors, plus one 'further' member who must not come from a background related in any way to either shareholder or employee interests.

In practice, any system which is so delicately tuned will in time begin to cough and splutter – as the German sytem is already doing. It will end up with bronchitis, which is infectious if you get too close. The only valuable lesson from German practice is that works councils can play a productive role. These can be formed, if the employees wish, in all companies with more than five employees. They act as a watchdog over employer–union agreements, and must be consulted or informed on matters such as safety, manpower and investment plans, production changes, and the general situation of the company. More controversially, they also have powers to give or withhold approval on working conditions, hours, wage scales, holidays, rules for engaging and dismissing employees, specific dismissals, new work methods, closures or reduced working, takeovers and mergers.

On the whole, common sense, and collective sense in the balancing of overall company interests with specifically worker-oriented interests, prevailed in West Germany until the politically-oriented Codetermination Act of 1976 introduced unnecessary new stresses, of which we have certainly not heard the last.

Danish Boards

The two-tier system applies if the company's capital exceeds Danish Kroner 400,000 (= ca. £30,000 in 1980), or if there are more than 50 employees. The two types of company are the public limited company (*Aktieselskab*, A/S) and the private limited company (*Anpartsselskab*, Aps).

With two tiers, the Board (*Bestyrelse*) ensures that there is a suitable organisation for the activities of the company, produces guidelines and instructions for management, and appoints the management.

The management (*Direktion*) conducts the daily management, and refers significant decisions to the Board. Division of functions between the two levels is loosely defined, and varies widely in practice. It may be defined in the articles. Both levels can represent the company to third parties, and can bind the company.

The articles may provide for a shareholders' committee, which supervises the administration of the company by both the Board and the management, and may take responsibility for appointing the Board away from the general meeting. Such committees are still rare.

The Board has a minimum of three Directors. Where there

are more than 50 employees, which is the case in around 3,000 companies, those employees can appoint two Directors only to the Board, irrespective of how many other Directors have been appointed by the shareholders. (In Sweden the limiting size is 25 employees.) These two Directors must have been employed by the company for at least a year, and are appointed for two years. They may be removed during that period by the employees. They may not participate in Board discussions on wages, labour relations, or labour conflicts, which makes one wonder just what they can contribute. As voting for these two Directors is by simple majority of all employees, 'blue-collar' workers will tend to predominate. When the worker Director reform was first introduced the blue- and white-collar categories commonly agreed to share the seats, one apiece; latterly the blue category has tended to take both. The Board is empowered to coopt a white-collar nominee if it feels such would be helpful, even when two blue-collar representatives have been elected. The white-collar nominee is then appointed by the shareholders.

Not all companies with more than 50 employees have chosen to elect worker Directors. Many, particularly the smallest, prefer the kind of consultation available through cooperation committees, where management and employees are equally represented. By an agreement between the Danish equivalent of the Trades Union Congress and the Employers' Federation, such committees can be formed in any company with more than 50 employees where either management or workers want it.

The Board may contain managers as Directors (in contrast to West German law) and about one-third do so. The Chief Executive of United Breweries, the Carlsberg/Tuborg combine, for example, is not a Board Director. The majority of the Board must be non-executive if the capital is over Danish Kroner 400,000. When the Board itself does not contain managers as Directors, it is quite common to find that the Chief Executive is 'coopted' to attend Board meetings, though without a vote. Managers in general have the right to attend and address the Board if they so request.

The Chairman of the Board (*Formand*) can be full time, i.e. effectively executive, but he cannot be a member of management.

Directors or managers who wilfully or negligently inflict loss on the company are liable for damages. Similarly with founders or auditors. Decision on taking such action is made by the general meeting, or by shareholders with at least 10 per cent of the equity.

The flexibility with which the Danes may apply their legislation has enabled them to operate their system smoothly, to date. In practice it lies half-way between the German two-tier structure and the UK's unitary system, in some aspects closer to the former, in others to the latter. In a strictly business sense, the Danes have long demonstrated exceptional skill in overcoming the severe disadvantage of having no native natural resources whatever, apart from their wits and professionalism. Alas, here too politically-oriented pressure for changes to shareholding structures is introducing un-productive new stresses to an economy already under siege.

French Boards

The articles of a French company determine whether a two-tier or unitary structure is applied, the latter being called the 'classical' system.

A limited company (*Société Anonyme*, SA, and broadly though not precisely the same as the British plc, and German AG) most commonly maintains a single tier. Similarly with a private limited company (*Société à responsabilité limitée*, Sàrl). There are 300,000 Sàrl and 100,000 SA.

1 The single-tier SA has a Board (*conseil d'administration*) of Directors (*administrateurs*) and is managed by a président elected by the Board from among its members. The Board delegates most of its powers to him, and he represents the company to third parties. He cannot be president of more than two French SAs, excluding affiliated companies. A general manager (*directeur général*) can be appointed to assist the president, and he may or may not be a Director. His powers are the same as those of the president, and there can be two general managers if the capital exceeds 500,000 francs. There are 3–12

Directors, and none may hold more than 8 directorships. Up to one-third of the Directors may be employees (of any level) and they must have been employed by the company for at least two years. Directors are appointed in general meeting; general managers are appointed by the Board on the suggestion of the president. Directors are liable for damages in cases of mismanagement, and action can be brought by shareholders representing only 5 per cent of the equity. They can also be held responsible for the entire excess of liabilities over assets if the company becomes bankrupt as a result of demonstrated mismanagement. (One can usefully compare with the current comparatively lenient practice in the UK.)

2   In the two-tier alternative there is a supervisory board (*conseil de surveillance*) and a directorate (*directoire*). The supervisory Board appoints and supervises the directorate, and may appoint general managers to assist the president. It contains 3–13 members, with the same limit on number of directorships, and the same range of liabilities, as in the single-tier system. The directorate, or 'management board', acts as a body, with 1–5 members. It has a president, but no special powers are delegated to him. No person can be a member of the directorate of more than two French SAs, and no member of a directorate can be a member of the same company's supervisory Board. The directorate must report at least once every three months to the supervisory Board.

3   The Sàrl is managed by managers (*gérants*) rather than by a Board, but they have similar powers and duties to those of Directors.

4   The French also permit the formation of an economic cooperation group (*groupement d'intérêt économique*), which is a loose grouping of persons, companies and/or other organisations composed to serve the economic interests of its members. It is a legal entity, not just a grouping of bodies tied to each other by a

contract, though there will normally be such a contract defining the objectives and operations of the grouping. It is mainly used for cooperation between companies to assist them in exporting, research, materials processing, or similar, and it may not operate for outsiders, nor itself operate for profit. It is managed by *administrateurs*; multiple votes are possible (a more influential or more interested member may have more votes than a lesser member); there is unlimited liability for debts incurred within the grouping's objectives.

In February 1975 the French 'Committee on the Reform of the Enterprise' produced a report, known as the Sudreau Report. This proposed a large number of changes to French corporate structures, including:

an extension of employee representation on single and two-tier Boards;
full voting rights for employee representatives;
an extension of employee participation schemes;
a reduction in the number of directorships which can be held;
a more frequent renewal of Board membership;
the separation of the roles of Chairman and Chief Executive;
plannned successions from the age of 60 years; and
far-reaching rights for information and consultation for works councils, especially in holding and multinational companies.

The report received an understandably varied reception, and its proposals have been largely left on the shelf, pro tem.

Acknowledgement: The major source of legal data for Appendix II is Dr Peter Meinhardt's *Company Law in Europe*, Gower, 1978. The writer, however, is responsible for operational details, and for opinions expressed.

Appendix III
Recommended reading

Legal

1 Your company's memorandum and articles of association.
2 The Companies Acts of 1948, 1967, 1976 and 1980.
3 Peter Loose, *The Company Director, his functions, powers and duties*, Jordans. The fifth edition is dated 1975, but a separate September 1980 Supplement brings the material up to date.
4 Dr Peter Meinhardt, *Company Law in Europe*, Gower, third edition 1981.

Statistics and commentary on the Board in the UK

1 *Boards of Directors Study, 1980*, Korn/Ferry International, London. Compiled from questionnaires to *Times 1000* companies.
2 *The Responsibilities and Contribution of Non-Executive Directors on the Boards of UK Companies*, Booz-Allen & Hamilton/Institute of Directors, 1979. Compiled from questionnaires to *Times 1000* companies, plus small companies which are members of the Institute of Directors.
3 Christopher Brookes, *Boards of Directors in British Industry*, Research Paper No. 7, Department of Employment, 1979. Includes some analyses of Boardroom practice.
4 *Boards of Directors in Small/Medium-Sized Private Companies*, Information Summary 149, 1970, BIM. Compiled from questionnaires to companies with up to 500 employees.

5   *The Board of Directors*, Management Survey Report
    No. 10, 1972, BIM. Compiled from questionnaires.
6   Richard Whitley, *Commonalities and Connections among
    Directors of Large Financial Institutions*, Manchester
    Business School, 1974.

Statistics and commentary on the Board in the US

1   *Board of Directors*, Annual Study 1980, Korn/Ferry
    International, Los Angeles. Compiled from
    questionnaires.

Non-executive Directors

1 (UK)   *The Independent Director in the British Company*,
         Korn/Ferry International, London, 1979.
         Mainly qualitative summary of round-table
         discussions.
2 (UK)   R. I. Tricker/Deloitte Haskins & Sells, *The
         Independent Director*, Tolley, 1978. Extensive
         bibliography.
3 (US)   Noyes E. Leech and Robert H. Mundheim,
         The Outside Director in the Public Corporation,
         Korn/Ferry International, 1976. Qualitative
         commentary on the non-executive in the US.
4 (US)   Joseph W. Barr, 'The Role of the Professional
         Director', in *Harvard Business Review*, May–
         June 1976.
5 (US)   Marvin Chandler, 'It's Time to Clean up the
         Boardroom', in *Harvard Business Review*,
         September–October 1975.

General

1   Peter F. Drucker, *Management: Tasks, Responsibilities,
    Practices*, Harper & Row/Heinemann, 1974.
    Especially chapter 52: 'Needed: An Effective Board'.

2   Myles L. Mace, *Directors, Myth and Reality*, Harvard, 1971. Especially 'Conclusions'.
3   John Argenti, *Corporate Collapse*, McGraw-Hill, 1976.
4   George Bull (ed.), *Director's Handbook*, McGraw-Hill, 1977. Wide range of separately authored articles.
5   *Guidelines for Directors*, Institute of Directors, 1973; 3rd revision March, 1980.

Industrial and commercial performance data

1   Professor G. H. Lawson, 'The Measurement of Corporate Profitability on a Cash-flow Basis', in *The International Journal of Accounting*, vol. 16, no. 1, 1980.
2   *Size Report*, C & D Partners, 1979. Performance data on the 4,000 largest companies in the UK.
3   *Industrial Performance Analysis* (annual) and 150 separate *Sector Reports* (annual) by ICC Business Ratios, London. Also on Prestel. Company and comparative performance data.
4   *Jordan's Surveys* on approximately 60 industries, Jordans, London. Structural and financial data.
5   *Top 2000 Private Companies*; *Top 1000 Foreign-Owned Companies in the UK*; *Top 1000 Quoted Companies*, Jordans, London, annual.

Index